T. Scott Cunningham, Hope Davis and Kent Lanier in a scene from the Vineyard Theatre production of "Pterodactyls." Set design by James Youmans.

PTERODACTYLS

BY NICKY SILVER

DRAMATISTS
PLAY SERVICE
INC.

PTERODACTYLS
Copyright © 1994, Nicky Silver

All Rights Reserved

PTERODACTYLS was produced by Vineyard Theatre (Douglas Aibel, Artistic Director; Jon Nakagawa, Managing Director), in New York City, in October, 1993. It was directed by David Warren; the scene design was by James Youmans; the costume design was by Teresa Snider-Stein; the lighting design was by Donald Holder; the sound design was by Brian Hallas; the fight director was Rick Sordelet; the production stage manager was Karen Loftus, and the sculpture was by Jim Gary. The cast was as follows:

TODD DUNCAN .... T. Scott Cunningham
EMMA DUNCAN .... Hope Davis
TOMMY MCKORCKLE .... Kent Lanier
GRACE DUNCAN .... Kelly Bishop
ARTHUR DUNCAN .... Dennis Creaghan

ACT ONE

"Is It Any Wonder I Can't Remember A Thing?"

Setting
The elegant living room of the Duncan family of Main Line, Philadelphia.

Time
Summer

ACT TWO

Scene One: "An Appropriate Gift" — Autumn
Scene Two: "A Walk in the Park" — Winter

CHARACTERS

TODD DUNCAN, 23
EMMA DUNCAN, 20, Todd's sister
TOMMY McKORCKLE, 22, Emma's fiancé
GRACE DUNCAN, 45-50, Todd and Emma's mother
ARTHUR DUNCAN, 45-50, Todd and Emma's father

AUTHOR'S NOTE

PTERODACTYLS is a play about, among other things, systems of denial and the price they carry in the world today. As such, most of the characters have a specific method of denial (memory loss, alcoholism, abstraction, etc.) and as a group, the Duncan family lives in a grand mechanism of denial: farce. Drawing freely from theatrical worlds suggested by Phillip Barry and Kaufman and Hart, they muddle along never noticing a threat until it's too late. This is not to suggest that the actors can perform even the silliest-seeming moments with anything less than the strongest commitment. No matter how manic or absurd the action, it is based in real need. If it is not, the moments when a darker truth pokes through will fall flat. And the ending, when all efforts to maintain a bright facade have passed, will seem to come from nowhere. We were very blessed in the original production with actors who instinctively understood this juxtaposition of broad comedy and utter despair. What matters is that these conflicting spirits not become muddy. The hard-edged humor should not be softened, nor the rage diluted to achieve a homogenous texture. The texture is not intended to be homogenous. It should be disturbing, and even shocking when harsh reality intrudes.

It is also very important that the character of Todd, who has no comically exaggerated denial mechanism, *not* be portrayed as "better" than the others. His actions are, objectively, amoral. He may be our way into the play, but he must not be interpreted as superior. That approach would instill an atmosphere of righteousness and throw the play out of balance. Only when Todd is sufficiently cruel will we feel for those he victimizes. Mind you his cruelty need not be overt, I simply want to indicate that Todd is no more heroic than the other characters.

Lastly, as with all plays in today's economy, *Pterodactyls* took a great effort, by many people, to get to the stage. It may be inappropriate to do so here, but I would feel remiss if I did not take this opportunity to thank, in print, those who encouraged me and nurtured the play from first draft to production. They include: Michael Traum, Douglas Aibel, Tim Sanford, Nick Martin, James Bart Upchurch, John Guare, Bruce Whitacre, Nancy Turner Hensley, Howard Shalwitz, Chuck Coggins, David Warren and the very brilliant original cast.

PTERODACTYLS

ACT ONE

"Is It Any Wonder I Can't Remember A Thing?"

The stage is dark. A pool of light comes up on Todd Duncan. Dressed casually, in clothes obviously much, much too big for him, he stands at an easel, on which is propped a map of the earth. He carries a pointer. He addresses the audience.

TODD.   In the beginning, there were dinosaurs. Lots of dinosaurs. And they were big. They were very, very large — in comparison to man they were. They were huge. And there were many different kinds. There were cerotops and stegosauruses. There was the tyrannosaurus and the pterodactyl. And they lived, not in harmony, roaming the earth at will, raping, as it were, the planet and pillaging without regard. And, and um ... uh. *(He looses his place and quickly checks his pockets for notes.)* Um, I seem to have forgotten my notes. I'm sorry. I thought I left them in my pocket. Maybe I wasn't supposed to wear this. Maybe I left them on the table. Maybe I — oh well, it doesn't matter now. I don't have them. That's the point. I think I remember most of it — Maybe I left them — it doesn't matter. Where was I? Oh, yes. It got cold. That's right, it got very, very cold and all the dinosaurs died. They all died. At once. It got cold and they died. And the land masses shifted and arranged themselves into the pattern we see now on the map. Basically. I think. There weren't any divisions for countries or states or anything, and I'm sure California was bigger, but it resembled what's on the map. During the cold spell, which is generally referred to as "the ice age" — or maybe it was before the ice age, or after it — I can't remember — but life started spontaneously. In a lake.

7

Here, I think. *(He indicates the sea of Japan.)* And amoebas multiplied and became fish — don't ask me how — which evolved into monkeys. And then one day, the monkeys stood up, erect, realized they had opposing thumbs and developed speech. Thus, Mankind was born. Here. *(He indicates Africa.)* Some people liked Africa, so they stayed there and became black. Some people left, looking for something, and became Europeans. And the Europeans forgot about the Africans and made countries and Queen Elizabeth executed her own half-sister Mary Queen of Scots. Some Europeans were Jewish, but most were Christians of some kind, Jesus having been born some time prior — oops, I forgot that. I'm sorry. Jesus was born. And there were other religions too, but I can't remember much about them, so I'm sure they weren't very important. During the Renaissance people got very fat. Picasso sculpted "David," Marco Polo invented pizza, Columbus discovered the new world and Gaetan Dugas discovered the fountain of youth. Europeans imported tea, to drink, and Africans to do their work. Edison invented the telephone. Martha Graham invented modern dance. Hitler invented fascism and Rose Kennedy invented nepotism. Orson Wells made *Citizen Kane* and mothers loved their children, who rebelled, when the sun shined most of the time, except when it rained and there was a rhythm to our breathing. There was an order to the world. And I was born here. *(He indicates Philadelphia.)* I give you this brief summary of events. this overview, so you'll have some perspective. I'm sure I got some of it wrong, I've lost my notes, but it's basically the idea. And I wanted you to have, I think, some sense of history. *(He picks up the easel and exits. The lights come up on the living room of the Duncan family. The decor suggests, not just money, but breeding. There is a sofa, end tables, wing-back chairs, fresh flowers and four exits. One to the outside world, one to the kitchen, a pair of French doors reveal a terrace and the yard beyond. Stairs lead to the second floor. Tommy is standing behind Emma, kissing her.)*

EMMA. I'm nervous

TOMMY. Don't be.

EMMA. I don't feel well.

TOMMY. You smell like wet feathers

EMMA. I can't breath.

TOMMY. Your neck tastes like licorice.

EMMA. I'm going to suffocate.

TOMMY. Your hair tastes like marzipan.

EMMA. Don't eat my hair.

TOMMY. Say that again.

EMMA. Don't eat my hair.

TOMMY. Your voice is like Mozart!

EMMA. I feel like there's a brick behind my eyes.

TOMMY. Your voice is Ravel.

EMMA. Do you have a decongestant?

TOMMY. It's Wagner!

EMMA. Some Vapo-Rub?

TOMMY. You are the Venus vomited forth by the sea on the shell of a clam.

EMMA. Ick.

TOMMY. Have I upset you?

EMMA. Oh no. Although I do find the use of the word "vomit" disturbing.

TOMMY. I'm sorry.

EMMA. In a romantic setting.

TOMMY. I can't do anything right. I don't know why I try.

EMMA. Do you have an antihistamine?

TOMMY. I'm a dope.

EMMA. Now I've depressed you.

TOMMY. You haven't.

EMMA. I have. I can tell.

TOMMY. It's not you. It's not your fault. I get depressed alot.

EMMA. Do you have a Drixoral?

TOMMY. Almost anything can set me off. If my coffee's too hot or too cold. If the sky is cloudy or the sun is too bright. Sometimes I just slip into an uncontrollable funk for no reason at all.

EMMA. I never noticed.

TOMMY. I've hidden it. I thought you'd find it unattractive.

EMMA. How long does it last?

TOMMY. A moment.

EMMA. Oh. (*Pause.*) How are you now?

TOMMY. I'm fine.

EMMA. That's good.

TOMMY. But my tooth —

EMMA. What?

TOMMY. I've got a terrible toothache.

EMMA. That's too bad.

TOMMY. It's nothing.

EMMA. Do you think there's something caught?

TOMMY. I floss.

EMMA. Just decay.

TOMMY. I think it's a wisdom tooth.

EMMA. I have some Darvon in my purse.

TOMMY. Why?

EMMA. I get leg cramps.

TOMMY. I never noticed.

EMMA. I suffer in silence. How's your toothache?

TOMMY. Spreading down my arm.

EMMA. I've lost sensation in my hip.

TOMMY. From what?

EMMA. I don't know.

TOMMY. My hand is twitching, isn't it?

EMMA. No.

TOMMY. It's nerves.

EMMA. It's not twitching.

TOMMY. You just can't see it.

EMMA. If it were twitching I could see it.

TOMMY. It's twitching internally.

EMMA. If you say so.

TOMMY. Don't patronize me.

EMMA. I wouldn't. I love you.

TOMMY. Really?

EMMA. Yes. I think about you all the time. I try to read, or brush my hair but all I think about is you. Sometimes I say your name over and over again, under my breath. No one can hear me, but I don't care. It just feels good to say it.

TOMMY. Thanks.

EMMA.   Try it sometime. You'll see. *(Grace enters, carrying shopping bags.)*
GRACE.   Flo!
EMMA.   Mother. I'm so glad you're home —
GRACE.   Help me with these, would you? It's hot as an oven and my arm's asleep. *(Emma takes Grace's bags. Seeing Tommy for the first time.)* Oh. Hello.
EMMA.   Mother, I'd like you to meet —
GRACE.   I must look unbearable. The sidewalk is melting and I would swear that I actually saw someone fry an egg.
TOMMY.   It's very warm.
GRACE.   Goodness, I'm exhausted. I've had the most horrible day.
EMMA.   Mother —
GRACE.   I've been to the city — I picked up the most cunning little black sheath, Dolce & Gabana, and a sweet suit, so Isey Miyake!
EMMA.   Mother —
GRACE.   *(Adjusting her hair and makeup.)* I used to enjoy shopping. When I married your father it was a real event to go into the city, have lunch in the sunshine, in Rittenhouse Square. Everyone was well-mannered and well-groomed. People wore hats. Now. Now, the Square is filled with hobos needing a bath and a companion. Really. They just stagger about in the sunlight, dirty and talking to themselves about the fall of communism and what-not. I don't know. I tried, but I couldn't follow a word of it. They all just want money, anyway. You can't encourage them. Give them a coin, they talk your ear off.
EMMA.   Mother.
GRACE.   *(Finished her work.)* Yes, dear?
EMMA.   This is Tommy McKorckle — *(To Tommy.)* stand up straight.
TOMMY.   How do you do?
GRACE.   It's nice to meet you. Emma so seldom brings around boys.
EMMA.   Mother.
TOMMY.   The pleasure is mine.
GRACE.   Isn't that charming? He's charming. You're charm-

ing.

TOMMY. I like your dress.

GRACE. *(Ringing a small bell on an end table.)* Thank you. I need a hot drink and a cold bath — or vice versa.

TOMMY. It suits you.

GRACE. "A+" for charm.

EMMA. Mother, I'd like to talk to you.

GRACE. Oh. Emma. This may not be the day. I'm exhausted.

TOMMY. Maybe we should wait.

EMMA. Tommy.

GRACE. Look at me — if you dare — I've perspired through my clothing. I'm a wreck.

TOMMY. Not at all.

GRACE. You're sweet. I need a quick drink and a long bath, or the other way around — *(She rings the bell again.)* Where's Flo?

EMMA. Who?

GRACE. Flo, dear. Where is she?

EMMA. I don't know anyone named "Flo." Is she with you?

GRACE. The maid. Flo, our maid.

EMMA. Flo?

GRACE. Flo. Florence. You remember Flo. Wears wigs, walks with a limp.

EMMA. *(Discouraged.)* Oh I don't know.

GRACE. You must excuse my daughter, Mr. —

TOMMY. McKorckle.

GRACE. Yes. She forgets things.

EMMA. I write things down. I try to concentrate. But facts run through me like Chinese food.

TOMMY. I think it's sweet.

GRACE. Do you. Really? Lord, I'm thirsty. *(Grace rings again.)* Where could she be? I hope she's all right. I hope nothing's happened to her.

EMMA. *(Asserting herself.)* We have to talk, Mother.

GRACE. Can't it wait?

EMMA. No.

GRACE. I'm exhausted and I seem to be without a staff.

TOMMY.   Maybe tomorrow.

EMMA.   We have to assert ourselves.

GRACE.   Oh what is it?

EMMA.   Well, I wanted you to meet Tommy —

GRACE.   And I have. May I bathe now?

EMMA.   *(Blurting it out.)* Because we're going to get married! *(Pause.)*

GRACE.   Pardon me?

EMMA.   That's it. That's what I wanted to say. That's what I said. We're getting married.

TOMMY.   Assuming you approve, and Mr. Duncan too, of course.

EMMA.   Tommy?

GRACE.   I see.

EMMA.   And, well, that's what I wanted to tell you. *(Grace sits.)* Well?

GRACE.   Well what?

EMMA.   What do you think?

GRACE.   *(After a moment.)* How long have you known my daughter. Mr. —

TOMMY.   McKorckle.

EMMA.   Call him Timmy.

TOMMY.   Tommy.

EMMA.   Sorry.

TOMMY.   Three weeks.

GRACE.   That's not very long.

EMMA.   It's long enough.

GRACE.   I see. Do you drink?

EMMA.   Mother.

GRACE.   I don't trust a man who drinks. My father's brother drank and suffered fits of kleptomania.

TOMMY.   I don't drink.

GRACE.   Emma? Have you been doing things you oughtn't?

EMMA.   Of course not.

TOMMY.   Socially, sometimes.

GRACE.   You wouldn't remember if you had.

TOMMY.   Wine with dinner.

GRACE.   Let me see your hands.

13

TOMMY.   Pardon me?

GRACE.   *(Inspecting Tommy.)* You don't wear jewelry, do you? No necklace under your shirt?

TOMMY.   No Ma'am.

GRACE.   I don't trust a man with a necklace.

EMMA.   He doesn't wear jewelry, Mother.

TOMMY.   Does a watch count?

GRACE.   Men who wear jewelry are repulsive. It's a sign of weakness. It's not natural. Wouldn't you agree?

TOMMY.   I never thought about it.

GRACE.   Some men have to wear medic-alert necklaces. That's understandable. They're epileptic, or allergic to penicillin. But beyond that, men in jewelry are aberrations, criminals against nature. They're freaks and we want nothing to do with them.

TOMMY.   I don't wear any jewelry.

GRACE.   Thank goodness.

EMMA.   Why aren't you happy for me mother?

GRACE.   I am. This just comes as a shock. One day you're sitting in your room, all by yourself, not a friend in the world, and the next you're getting married — *(To Tommy.)* tell me something about yourself.

TOMMY.   I think I can make Emma happy. I know she makes me happy. From the moment I saw her—

GRACE.   Tell me about your family.

TOMMY.   I have no family.

GRACE.   Oh. Why's that?

TOMMY.   I'm an only child.

GRACE.   Oh?

TOMMY And my parents died when I was six.

GRACE.   That is too bad. An accident?

TOMMY.   Heart attacks.

GRACE.   How odd.

EMMA.   He was raised by acrobats!

GRACE.   I'm only taking an interest.

EMMA.   What difference does it make about his family?

GRACE.   Please. I'm not judging. I'm only asking. You tell me you plan to marry this young man. Now, what kind of

14

mother would I be if I showed only a cursory interest?

TOMMY.   It's all right. I was raised by nuns at the orphanage on City Line.

GRACE.   How cunning of you.

EMMA.   Must you be so condescending?

GRACE.   I have no idea what you mean. Do you know what she means?

TOMMY.   I lived with the nuns for twelve years.

GRACE.   Were they kind?

TOMMY.   Not really.

GRACE.   I'm so sorry.

TOMMY.   But the priests were giving.

GRACE.   I bet they were.

EMMA.   What do you mean?

GRACE.   I've heard stories.

EMMA.   What stories?

TOMMY.   The nuns kept mostly to themselves.

GRACE.   And now?

TOMMY.   I'm sure they're still involved. They had inseverable ties.

GRACE.   No, no. You.

EMMA.   What kind of stories?

TOMMY.   I've broken off completely. Although I still get letters from Father O'Hara, who seems fixated.

GRACE.   That's not what I meant.

EMMA.   My stomach hurts.

GRACE.   What do you do now?

EMMA.   There's something in my stomach.

GRACE.   You do work?

TOMMY.   I'm a waiter.

GRACE.   *(As if she does not recognize the word.)* A waiter?

TOMMY.   At Salad City.

GRACE.   I'm unfamiliar.

TOMMY.   On Suburban Square.

EMMA.   That's where we met.

GRACE.   How touching.

TOMMY.   It's very nice, really. We do a big lunch trade. Salads mostly.

GRACE. I assumed.

TOMMY. I was just a bus-boy then.

EMMA. He scratched and clawed his way to waiter.

TOMMY. I have ambitions.

GRACE. It's obvious. You have winning ways.

EMMA. You may not be able to tell by looking at him now, Mother, but Tommy's going to be very important.

GRACE. Head Waiter?

TOMMY. There are *no* head waiters in Salad City.

GRACE. I don't mean to be unenthusiastic. Really I don't. I've no intentions of squashing your romance, but Emma, I have to say, I have my doubts.

EMMA. Why can't you be supportive?

GRACE. I just don't think a waiter is for you.

EMMA. I hate you.

GRACE. My daughter is used to the finer things. Godiva chocolates. Prescription pills.

TOMMY. I won't be a waiter forever.

EMMA. You just don't want me to be happy!

TOMMY. I have plans.

GRACE. Thank goodness. What are they?

TOMMY. I'm thinking of going into law. Or medicine. Or maybe banking.

GRACE. Mr. Duncan is in banking.

TOMMY. But what I really want to do is direct.

EMMA. Tommy's a genius.

TOMMY. I love the movies.

GRACE. I never go.

TOMMY. You're kidding!

GRACE. Sex and violence, violence and sex. Bare breasts and imitation butter.

TOMMY. *(Passionate.)* Have you ever seen *Hiroshima Mon Amour?*

GRACE. I missed it.

TOMMY. I have vision!

EMMA. Mother. I love Tommy. And I intend to marry him.

GRACE. I see. *(Pause.)* Well, first thing we'll have to do is get you out of that restaurant. It really won't do. Where do

you live?
TOMMY.   When I left the orphanage. I took a furnished room on Market Street.
GRACE.   I see.
TOMMY.   But I had to give it up, tips not being what I'd hoped for.
EMMA.   They expect him to wear tight jeans and keep his shirt unbuttoned.
TOMMY.   *(Ashamed.)* Did you ever see *The Night Porter?*
GRACE.   No. And now?
TOMMY.   I have a lean-to on Lancaster Pike.
GRACE.   Oh.
TOMMY.   It's not bad. It's nice really — except when it rains.
GRACE.   Hmmmm. *(Pause.)* I know! You'll stay here! With us!
TOMMY.   Well —
EMMA.   That's a wonderful idea!
TOMMY.   I'm afraid I couldn't do that.
GRACE.   Why not?
TOMMY.   I have my pride.
EMMA.   Tommy!
TOMMY.   *(Proud.)* Did you ever see *The Grapes of Wrath?*
GRACE.   I'll tell you what — you can earn your keep!
TOMMY.   Doing what?
GRACE.   Well, Flo seems to be in absentia. You can be the maid!
TOMMY.   I don't know —
EMMA.   *(To Grace.)* You're a genius!
TOMMY.   I don't think —
GRACE.   Perhaps Mr. Duncan could find you something at the bank, but I hate to ask him — he's been overwrought lately. If you prove yourself as the maid then he'll have to give you a job!
TOMMY.   Couldn't we just —
GRACE.   It's settled. You need a job and I need a servant!
TOMMY.   But —
GRACE.   No, no! I've decided. And when I decide some-

17

thing I decide it. Now, come along with me and we'll see if that old Flo left any uniforms in her closet — you'll love the servants' quarters. Pale blue with little ducks on the baseboard — then you can draw me a bath!

TOMMY.   Emma!

GRACE.   *(Ushering Tommy off.)* You can have Mondays and every other Sunday off. Unless of course we're entertaining. Can you make Bananas Foster? Flo made a divine Bananas Foster!

TOMMY.   Of course not.

GRACE.   *(Exiting.)* It's easy! You take several ripe bananas and a bottle of brandy, sauté in butter, halve the bananas, flambé and serve, at once, à la môde. *(Grace and Tommy are gone. Emma goes to her purse and takes a pill. She addresses the audience. As she speaks, Todd enters, unnoticed by her, through the terrace doors.)*

EMMA.   I know I shouldn't. But one can't hurt, and dear God I'm in continual pain. My skin is killing me. I feel as if this weren't my skin at all. It's someone else's skin. It's the skin of a tiny child and it's been stretched over my body. I'm sorry, I'm Emma Duncan. Welcome. I don't mind telling you I'm glad that's over. Mother can be so over-bearing. I know she means well. I know she loves me. I know it, I know it, I know it, I know it. But that doesn't make her any easier to take and Tommy doesn't have much self-confidence. But he does have beautiful hair and lips like pudding. Doesn't he? I think I love him very much. I dream about him every night —

TODD.   Hello.

EMMA.   *(Startled.)* What?!

TODD.   I said hello.

EMMA.   Where did you come from?

TODD.   I walked from the train station.

EMMA.   *(She is nervous and afraid of him.)* How did you get in here?

TODD.   I just want to lie down.

EMMA.   I asked you a question!

TODD.   The door was open.

18

EMMA. That door is locked!

TODD. No it's not.

EMMA. What do you want?

TODD. I need a place to live. I need a place to sleep. I've been traveling so long. I've been walking forever.

EMMA. Don't sit down!

TODD. Everything's different.

EMMA. What are you talking about?

TODD. The furniture's different.

EMMA. Different from what?

TODD. The sofa is new.

EMMA. Do you want money? Is that what you want?

TODD. I don't want any money.

EMMA. Why are you staring at me?!

TODD. You look so different.

EMMA. Don't come at me —

TODD. You look beautiful.

EMMA. Get out of here!

TODD. Don't you recognize me?

EMMA. Just go please!

TODD. You don't remember me?

EMMA. We've never never met —

TODD. *(Approaching her.)* Of course we have.

EMMA. Stay away!

TODD. Don't be afraid.

EMMA. Stay where you are!

TODD. I'm your brother.

EMMA. I don't have a brother!

TODD. I've been away a long time.

EMMA. My stomach hurts.

TODD. But I'm back.

EMMA. My skin is too tight.

TODD. What's wrong with you?

EMMA. I don't have any brothers or sisters!

TODD. Look at me!

EMMA. My father'll be home soon! If you touch me he'll kill you!

TODD. Look at me Emma!

EMMA. He's the chief of police! He's a Nazi! He'll kill you!
TODD. *(Grabbing her.)* Think!
EMMA. Let me go!
TODD. Remember growing up!
EMMA. You're hurting me!
TODD. We played games!
EMMA. Oh, God! You're going to rape me aren't you! GOD! DADDY! GOD! HELP ME!
TODD. Think! *(She breaks free.)* Emma!?
EMMA. *(Threatening him with a letter opener.)* I don't know who you are, but get out of here or I'll kill you myself! I WILL!
TODD. I just needed a place to stay — *(Grace rushes on.)*
GRACE. Emma! What on earth's going — *(She see Todd.)* Todd?
TODD. Mother. *(Grace and Todd embrace.)*
EMMA. *(To herself.)* There's something wrong with me. There's something very wrong.
GRACE. Let me look at you!
TODD. How are you Mother?
GRACE. Emma, why didn't you tell me your brother —
EMMA. I don't have a brother!!
TODD. I'm home Mother.
EMMA. Who is this person?
GRACE. She forgets things.
EMMA. I'd remember a brother.
GRACE. Well, you'd think so — Todd, let me look at you.
EMMA. What's going on here?
GRACE. Oh think Emma. You remember Todd. Think! He went away five years ago to study sculpting?
EMMA. I don't think so.
GRACE. Think back. When you were twelve we went to Washington? We had a picnic. We sat on the lawn and ate sandwiches and grapes. You got amebic dysentery.
EMMA. Who did?
TODD. When you were ten we all went to London, for Christmas.
GRACE. We ate lard and salty beans.

20

TODD. We walked the bridge in the cold dank mist.

EMMA. I don't know what anyone's talking about!

GRACE. She represses.

TODD. She's lucky.

GRACE. What an ironic remark. Isn't your brother ironic?

EMMA. Who?

GRACE. Skip it — You look thin. Are you eating?

TODD. You mean right now?

GRACE. I meant in general.

TODD. Oh.

GRACE. It's wonderful to see you — How long can you stay — Your father'll be thrilled!

TODD. He will?

GRACE. He'll be home soon. He's at the bank.

TODD. On a Sunday?

GRACE. Is it Sunday?

EMMA. *(Out.)* Who are these people!?

GRACE. I was just saying to Nina Triten how I wish you'd come home for a visit. I was beginning to think you didn't like us. And now, here you are! You're a man! A grown up! Do I look different? I've just lost five pounds. I eat lemon zest and bib lettuce! Prisoners on death row eat better than I! — I've stopped smoking. That was three years ago. When Bunny Witton died of emphysema, I took it for a sign — You look well. Your clothes don't fit and I must admit they're dirty.

TODD. They're comfortable.

GRACE. We'll get you some new clothes. We'll go shopping first thing in the morning. Remember how we used to go shopping? You'll need a blazer. I saw a beautiful Byblos at Plage Tahiti — Where are my manners!? You must be starved! How did you get here? Would you like a drink?

TODD. No thank you.

EMMA. I would. *(Grace rings bell.)*

GRACE. Be honest. I look older, don't I? I shouldn't. I had my eyes done last August, but one's tighter than the other and now everyone thinks I'm winking at them all the time — I know! We'll have a party! How long can you stay?

TODD.   I don't think that's —

GRACE.   It's decided! I have decided. You'll be the guest of honor!

TODD.   I have AIDS.

GRACE.   *(After a moment.)* We'll have a buffet, that'll be nice. You give me a list of what you'd like. Or we could barbecue. That'd be sweet. I don't have any idea what you like anymore.

TODD.   I have AIDS. I need a bed and a place to live. I have AIDS.

GRACE.   *(Falling apart, plowing ahead.)* Your father can string up those paper lanterns. The one's we used at your sister's sweet sixteen. We still have them I think. I think they're in the attic. We packed them away. I think, with the Christmas ornaments.

TODD.   I need a pillow and some peace and quiet.

EMMA.   Who are you?

GRACE.   We'll serve champagne or punch, or something to drink.

TODD.   I have —

GRACE.   *(Her despair now shows.)* And the Beekmans'll come! Essie was always fond of you. She's married now. Gotten fat. Don't be shocked when you see her.

TODD.   I said —

GRACE.   I don't think she's happy really. She married a nice enough man. Very attractive. In real estate.

TODD.   I have AIDS.

GRACE.   I think he beats her.

TODD.   I have AIDS.

GRACE.   And the Plimptons.

TODD.   Listen to me.

GRACE.   *(Rather frenzied now.)* And the Weathertons — maybe we should cater! I don't know — I love planning a party! I feel I'm really in my element when I'm planning a party! We'll have music on the terrace! I'm most alive planning a party! You'll see, Todd, it'll be wonderful! It'll be beautiful! You're going to love it! You're just going to love it!

TODD.   I have AIDS. *(There is a blackout. Grace steps into a pool of light and addresses the audience.)*

GRACE. We were always very close and I thought Todd extremely gifted. He sculpted the gargoyles on the terrace, of course that was later. We didn't need to speak. Sometimes, we would just sit in the garden, reading not needing to speak. We would watch the leaves change color. *(Arthur joins her in the pool of light.)* It's Todd, Arthur.

ARTHUR. Who?

GRACE. Buzz. Talk to him.

ARTHUR. What's wrong?

GRACE. He's dying. *(Grace turns and slowly exits. After a moment, Arthur addresses the audience.)*

ARTHUR. When he was a boy, Buzz wanted to be a sports announcer on the radio. He loved the Philadelphia Phillies. He talked about them all the time. He said their names over and over again: Nick Etten and Danny Litwiler, Eddy Waitkus and his favorite, Granville Hamner. Buzz worshipped him. He saw the poetry in his name. Oh, that was me. Not Buzz. I liked the Phillies. Buzz drew alot. I think. Buzz was born a month after my father died and I was a little distracted. He never liked the Phillies, I did. But later, we had catches, on the yard. And like all little boys, Buzz looked up to me and idealized me. He admired me. He loves me and I love him. He's my son and my world and the most important thing in my life — did I say thing? I mean person. And I would do anything for him. Take any suffering. I would cut off my arm. I wouldn't cut off my arm. I know it's a figure of speech, but I wouldn't. I need my arms. He's not the most important person in my life. I do love him, but I said that, didn't I? *(The lights come up. Todd is dragging a large sack in from the terrace.)* Buzz?!

TODD. Yes?

ARTHUR. What are you doing?

TODD. I've been in the yard.

ARTHUR. What?

TODD. I fell asleep on the sofa, I thought I'd never wake up. But I had strange dreams, so I went out for some air. *(Todd spills the contents of the sack onto the floor. It is dozens of bones.)*

ARTHUR.   What is that?

TODD.   There was something sticking up, out of the ground. I dug it up.

ARTHUR.   This is garbage.

TODD.   These are bones.

ARTHUR.   So, a dog buried bones.

TODD.   We don't have a dog.

ARTHUR.   Maybe your sister.

TODD.   *(Sorting through the bones, on the floor.)* I think this house was built on a burial ground.

ARTHUR.   So what?

TODD.   Or maybe there's been a murder.

ARTHUR.   What are you talking about?

TODD.   Or maybe these are fossils.

ARTHUR.   Put them away.

TODD.   I'm going to find out. I'm going to put them together.

ARTHUR.   I'd like to talk to you.

TODD.   *(Fitting the bones together.)* Talk.

ARTHUR.   Your mother tells me ...

TODD.   What?

ARTHUR.   She says you're dying.

TODD.   *(Ignoring Arthur, pulling more bones from the sack.)* Does she?

ARTHUR.   She's very upset.

TODD.   Is she?

ARTHUR.   Of course.

TODD.   She registers it oddly.

ARTHUR.   Listen to me.

TODD.   *(Not looking.)* I am listening.

ARTHUR.   She says you're going to die.

TODD.   We're all going to die.

ARTHUR.   Is it true?

TODD.   *(Looks at Arthur.)* Is what true?

ARTHUR.   Are you dying?

TODD.   *(Returning to his work.)* No.

ARTHUR.   Is this a joke? I don't find it funny.

TODD.   I never said I was dying.

ARTHUR.   Your mother said —

TODD.   I have AIDS. So what? I have no symptoms. I am asymptomatic. I'm healthy. I'm strong. I'm not dying.

ARTHUR.   Is there something you want?

TODD.   I'd like a Diet Coke.

ARTHUR.   I'd like us to be close.

TODD.   Uh-huh.

ARTHUR.   I'd like us to be friends Buzz. I'd like us to share things.

TODD.   Such as?

ARTHUR.   I don't know. You're my son.

TODD.   Uh-huh.

ARTHUR.   Buzzy, do you remember when you were ten? Your sister was eight. She was very sick, in the hospital. You were in a play in school. Do you remember that, Buzzboy?

TODD.   What was the play?

ARTHUR.   *Oliver.*

TODD.   It was *The Birthday Party,* by Harold Pinter.

ARTHUR.   Is that a musical about British pick-pockets and lovable street urchins?

TODD.   It's about a man pursued by mysterious strangers on his birthday, until he is driven to rape.

ARTHUR.   Really?

TODD.   Yes.

ARTHUR.   I remember urchins.

TODD.   You're mistaken.

ARTHUR.   Who did you play?

TODD.   The rapist.

ARTHUR.   You were ten.

TODD.   It was a private school.

ARTHUR.   I never cared for Pinter. I like *Oliver.* I like a nice story with a song. Don't you?

TODD.   What's the point?

ARTHUR.   I left the hospital the minute your sister was out of surgery. The minute they said she'd be OK I rushed to your school to see the second act. I'd missed the first.

TODD.   Thus your confusion as to the subject matter.

ARTHUR. You played a rapist?

TODD. In the sixth grade.

ARTHUR. That can't have been healthy. But I remember, you looked so cute. I was standing in the back and I was so proud.

TODD. I raped with aplomb.

ARTHUR. Don't sully the story — I remember it so clearly. I thought, "My daughter is safe, and my son is up there, on that stage, with all the other fathers looking, and watching." I felt we were close. It was a wonderful moment. Can't we be again?

TODD. What?

ARTHUR. Close.

TODD. We're close.

ARTHUR. No we're not, Buzzy.

TODD. Todd.

ARTHUR. Not really.

TODD. I don't know what you want.

ARTHUR. I'm your father.

TODD. So?

ARTHUR. We should do things together. Why can't you just try? Why can't you try to be my friend. Let me in? Confide in me.

TODD. I want to take a nap.

ARTHUR. How did you get this?

TODD. What?

ARTHUR. How did you get this disease?

TODD. That's none of your business.

ARTHUR. You can trust me, Buzz!

TODD. I don't think so.

ARTHUR. Try me!

TODD. I sat on a dirty toilet seat.

ARTHUR. I'm asking.

TODD. I ignored a chain letter.

ARTHUR. I want some rapport. When you were little we had catches, we had fun. Remember Sundays? They were your day. They were Buzzday. Let me in.

TODD. I fucked men.

ARTHUR. *(After a moment.)* Why?

TODD. If feels good.

ARTHUR. *(Hopeful.)* But they didn't fuck you?

TODD. It feels great. It feels better than great.

ARTHUR. It's all right. I'm not shocked.

TODD. *(As he continues, he speaks without anger.)* I fucked prostitutes I picked up on the street.

ARTHUR. That can't have been healthy.

TODD. I fucked women and men in bathrooms. In beds. On rooftops, in subways and basements and attics.

ARTHUR. I understand.

TODD. I took their fists up my ass and their cum down my throat. I gave blow jobs to people I never met, in dark rooms crowded with strangers. I buried my face in their asses, suffocating. I jerked off strangers, and wiped their cum on my face. And I knew what I was doing. I knew it was "not safe." And knowing drove me on. I was killing myself night after night. You want some rapport? Well, I can do nothing more to please you. *(Pause.)*

ARTHUR. Why are you here, Buzz?

TODD. This is my family.

ARTHUR. *(After a moment.)* I feel good about our talk. *(Todd reaches into the sack and pulls out a dinosaur skull.)*

TODD. Look.

ARTHUR. What?

TODD. It's a dinosaur! *(Todd holds up the skull to show Arthur.)*

ARTHUR. I'll see you at dinner. *(Arthur exits.)*

TODD. *(Addressing the audience.)* I was ten and, the night before the play, my mother came to see me. *(There is a light shift, in either angle or color. Todd lays down on the sofa. Grace enters. She carries a drink.)*

GRACE. Todd? *(No response.)* Todd are you sleeping? *(No response.)* Todd!

TODD. *(Groggy.)* What?

GRACE. Are you sleeping?

TODD. Mommy?

GRACE. Are you?

TODD. No.

GRACE.   That's good. I didn't want to wake you.

TODD.   What time is it?

GRACE.   Two-thirty.

TODD.   What do you want?

GRACE.   Would you like me to run your lines?

TODD.   I want to sleep.

GRACE.   Are you nervous about tomorrow?

TODD.   No.

GRACE.   (Sitting.) You're going to be wonderful. I was in plays when I was a girl. You and I are just alike. I'm sorry I won't be there. You know what's going on, don't you?

TODD.   I think so. You've crept into my room in the middle of the night.

GRACE.   I meant with your sister.

TODD.   Oh yes. She ate a shoe.

GRACE.   That's right. And it's stuck in her stomach. It's stuck in her bowel, and they have to operate to get it out.

TODD.   Why'd she eat it?

GRACE.   I have no idea. I don't understand anything she does. She's five.

TODD.   She's eight.

GRACE.   There were beets in the fridge. Perfectly good, delicious beets.

TODD.   I hate beets.

GRACE.   Me too. We're just alike.

TODD.   They make me sick.

GRACE.   (After a moment.) I'm so scared.

TODD.   What of?

GRACE.   Your sister's going to die.

TODD.   No she's not.

GRACE.   (Weeping.) I know she is! They're going to cut her open and she's going to die! God! Don't let her die!

TODD.   Can I have her records?

GRACE.   God is punishing me.

TODD.   There is no God.

GRACE.   There is and He punishes bad people — I dreamed I held a pillow over her face.

TODD.   I dreamed I was you.

28

GRACE.   If I was a good mother, I would've stopped her! I turn my back for a minute.

TODD.   Please cheer up.

GRACE.   You're so good. I can't cry — don't want to cry in front of your father. He needs me to be strong. He's frightened. He loves Emma. He prefers her to you, you know.

TODD.   I know.

GRACE.   I prefer you to me though.

TODD.   What?

GRACE.   I mean you to her. What did I say?

TODD.   Me to you.

GRACE.   Hold me.

TODD.   How?

GRACE.   Like this. *(She embraces him.)* I don't want Emma to die! I'll try to love her!

TODD.   Sssshhh. Sssshhh.

GRACE.   Play with my hair — I want to start over! I want her to be a baby again! I want to try again! I want another baby! I want to be a baby!

TODD.   Mommy.

GRACE.   *(Rising.)* Oh, I'm sorry. I'm sorry, it's late. I shouldn't burden you.

TODD.   It's all right.

GRACE.   I'm sorry. I just wanted to say good luck tomorrow.

TODD.   Thanks.

GRACE.   *(Cheery.)* Sleep tight. *(Grace exits.)*

TODD.   And I did. *(The lights revert back to normal. Todd exits onto the terrace. As he does, Tommy enters, with a feather duster, dressed as a maid as Emma descends the stairs.)*

EMMA.   Tommy, what are you doing?

TOMMY.   Dusting and waxing.

EMMA.   Can't it wait?

TOMMY.   This wood is parched.

EMMA.   You have all day.

TOMMY.   *(Paying no attention, happily cleaning.)* And a hectic schedule! I have to dust and polish, fetch your father's pinstripe from the cleaners, dip the silver and select a menu for dinner.

EMMA.   I'm having an asthma attack.

TOMMY.   And to tell you the truth, I'm out of ideas.

EMMA.   I'm running out of oxygen.

TOMMY.   Do you prefer Veal Diana to venison crêpes?

EMMA.   I'm suffocating.

TOMMY.   Of course everyone loves poultry.

EMMA.   The room is spinning.

TOMMY.   Except some people.

EMMA.   I'm going to faint.

TOMMY.   I could try a soufflé.

EMMA.   Everything is going black.

TOMMY.   I know! Fondue!

EMMA.   I'm not happy!!

TOMMY.   Don't you like fondue?

EMMA.   I don't think I've ever had it —

TOMMY.   Oh, you'll like it. It's fun. You take bread and very long forks and a pot of boiling cheese —

EMMA.   You've been here three weeks and everything's falling apart!

TOMMY.   *(Insulted.)* This place's never been so tidy!

EMMA.   *(Sadly.)* How can you wear that?

TOMMY.   Am I showing too much leg?

EMMA.   It's grotesque!

TOMMY.   I look good in black.

EMMA.   Something's very wrong here.

TOMMY.   I realize some men would find this get-up degrading and an insult to their masculinity, but I have to admit I find it liberating ... and oddly titillating.

EMMA.   I thought you'd rescue me. I never even see you.

TOMMY.   You're seeing me now.

EMMA.   You used to talk to me. You used to want me. You used to kiss me.

TOMMY.   I don't have time.

EMMA.   How long does it take?

TOMMY.   I have cheddar to melt.

EMMA.   You used to tell me I was beautiful. Don't you think I'm beautiful?

TOMMY.   *(Cleaning.)* Yeah, yeah, you're beautiful. You're hair's like candy, you're eyes like diamonds.

EMMA. *(Brightly.)* Let's discuss the wedding!

TOMMY. You talk. I'll dust.

EMMA. Do you hate me? Is that it?

TOMMY. I love you.

EMMA. I don't think so! You never even look at me! And aren't we ever going to have sex!?

TOMMY. Someone will hear you.

EMMA. I don't care. I don't want to die a virgin!

TOMMY. Hans Christian Anderson died a virgin.

EMMA. How do you know that?

TOMMY. I read it.

EMMA. Where?

TOMMY. In a book. And he brought happiness to millions of children all over the world.

EMMA. I don't want to bring happiness to millions of children all over the world!

TOMMY. Don't you like children?

EMMA. I want to experience sex! I'd like to have an orgasm! Is that so hard to understand?

TOMMY. It's a little self-centered.

EMMA. I'm a woman! I have breasts. I have a vagina. I want to use them.

TOMMY. *(Dusting.)* I see.

EMMA. Make love to me! Kiss me and kiss me in private places and make me forget that my skin is too small and every pore shrieks! Take me by force right here and now!

TOMMY. You're asking an awful lot.

EMMA. You say you love me. You know I love you —

TOMMY. You criticize me continually. You hate my outfit. How do you think that makes me feel? How do you expect me to have a healthy self-image if I don't feel good about the way I look?

EMMA. It's not bad really.

TOMMY. You don't mean that.

EMMA. Yes. I do. I like it. I'd like to borrow it.

TOMMY. You hate my cooking.

EMMA. That's not so. I loved last night's banana nut loaf.

TOMMY. You ate your eggs through a straw!

EMMA. Well they were raw.

TOMMY. They were soft.

EMMA. They were liquid — *(Todd enters from the terrace. carrying two dinosaur skeleton legs.)*

TODD. Look what I found!

EMMA and TOMMY. More bones. *(Todd sits and tries to piece the legs together with the other bones.)*

TODD. Oh, Tommy. I meant to tell you how much I enjoyed breakfast —

EMMA. I HATE YOU. I HATE EVERYONE! *(Emma exits.)*

TOMMY. I don't know what's gotten into her lately.

TODD. *(He is distracted. He pulls a book out from under the sofa and refers to it as he works with the bones.)* She was always high strung.

TOMMY. We're growing apart.

TODD. It happens to everyone.

TOMMY. It's happened to you?

TODD. Of course.

TOMMY. What did you do?

TODD. Watch.

TOMMY. That's all?

TODD. You can't fight the inevitable.

TOMMY. But I care about Emma! I love her! If anyone harmed her I'd kill them. We belong together.

TODD. And sex?

TOMMY. *(Casual.)* No thank you, I've just eaten.

TODD. I mean are you sexually compatible?

TOMMY. Well ... I don't know.

TODD. What do you mean?

TOMMY. We haven't actually had "sex."

TODD. Are you Mormon?

TOMMY. No.

TODD. Do you find her attractive?

TOMMY. She has beautiful eyes.

TODD. So do you.

TOMMY. Beautiful legs.

TODD. So do you.

TOMMY. Beautiful lips.

TODD. So do you.

TOMMY. Beautiful breasts!

TODD. So do — *(Pause.)* Then what is it?

TOMMY. Well, we've necked ... and so on.

TODD. Yes?

TOMMY. But the fact is — No, I'm sorry, I'm too embarrassed.

TODD. You can tell me. What is it? Trust me.

TOMMY. You see, I'm a little insecure.

TODD. What about?

TOMMY. Well, for one thing I don't think my penis is very big.

TODD. *(Sadly.)* Oh, I see.

TOMMY. But isn't that part of the human condition? I mean aren't all men, on some level, insecure about the size of their genitalia?

TODD. No.

TOMMY. I'm so humiliated! *(Todd places his hand on Tommy's crotch.)*

TODD. It feels ... big.

TOMMY. That's the feather duster.

TODD. I'm sorry.

TOMMY. But it's not just that. You see. I've never really had a woman.

TODD. Surely at the orphanage.

TOMMY. Just the priests. And they tied me up so all I had to do was shout the occasional "Hail Mary." They were easily satisfied. I never had to do anything. Now I'll have to do something!

TODD. You have nothing to worry about. I'll help you.

TOMMY. How can you? No one can. Sex is the loneliest arena.

TODD. Pretend I'm Emma.

TOMMY. Pardon me?

TODD. Pretend I'm Emma. I'll talk you through it.

TOMMY. Do you think we should? It might not be safe.

TODD. I'll be careful.

TOMMY.   I don't know. I've tried to forget my past and thi
seems oddly redundant.
TODD.   Just come here.
TOMMY.   *(Crossing to Todd.)* This won't involve harnesses o
holy water?
TODD.   Give me your hand.
TOMMY.   *(Doing so.)* All right.
TODD.   Put your hand on my waist.
TOMMY.   *(Doing so.)* Like we're dancing?
TODD.   And your other hand ...
TOMMY.   Yes?
TODD.   On my breast.
TOMMY.   What breast?
TODD.   *(Forceful.)* Imagine.
TOMMY.   *(Placing his hand.)* It's nice.
TODD.   Grab my nipple.
TOMMY.   Like that?
TODD.   Harder
TOMMY.   Like that?
TODD.   Harder. Just rip that mother-fucker off!!
TOMMY.   Doesn't that hurt.
TODD.   YES! YES! YES!
TOMMY.   It seems like a fetish.
TODD.   It's not! Women love this!
TOMMY.   What's next?
TODD.   Don't rush. Do this for a long time.
TOMMY.   How long?
TODD.   You'll know. And trade off, don't ignore the othe
one!!
TOMMY.   And then?
TODD.   Just shove her down on all fours like a dog an
degrade her!!
TOMMY.   *(Shocked.)* No!
TODD.   Yes!
TOMMY.   Shouldn't I build up to that?
TODD.   If you want.
TOMMY.   I do.
TODD.   All right, tell her she's pretty.

34

TOMMY.   You're pretty!

TODD.   Thanks. *(With that, Tommy clubs Todd to the floor with a grunt. There is a blackout. Emma rushes into a pool of light and addresses the audience.)*

EMMA.   I've had a memory! I don't think I saw it in a movie or a photograph. I think I remember it. Yes. It's my birthday. I'm seven, or twelve and it's a school day, so I have to go to school. But all the children have to make me a card in art class, and I get a cake in the cafeteria. I blow out my candles and I wish I were someone else. I wish I lived on a farm. I wish I were Pippi Longstocking. *(Arthur enters her pool of light.)*

ARTHUR.   Emma.

EMMA.   Hello, Daddy. I've had a memory!

ARTHUR.   Don't dwell.

EMMA.   Do you like Tommy?

ARTHUR.   Not very much.

EMMA.   Oh.

ARTHUR.   But if you love him, I — love him.

EMMA.   Is there something in your throat? You sound like you're choking.

ARTHUR.   I'm going to miss you very much.

EMMA.   You have a picture in your wallet.

ARTHUR.   It's not the same.

EMMA.   I'll miss you too, Daddy.

ARTHUR.   I have a wedding gift for you. *(He hands her a piece of gum.)*

EMMA.   It's a piece of gum.

ARTHUR.   When you were little you loved a piece of gum.

EMMA.   I did?

ARTHUR.   You were my little girl. *(He embraces her.)* When I came home from work, I'd give you some gum and you hugged me.

EMMA.   I did?

ARTHUR.   And I stroked your hair.

EMMA.   *(A little sick.)* You did?

ARTHUR.   And I whispered your name, and I loved you, and I kissed — *(Emma pushes away.)*

. Is it any wonder I can't remember a thing! *(Emma's [light] goes out. A light comes up on Grace.)*

[GRAC]E. My children were good children. Always well-be-[have]d and beautiful. When I had Emma, I had what's called [po]st-partum depression, so my mother came to stay with us and got on my nerves. Arthur and I were devoted parents. I read all the books on child-rearing. Todd cried a lot, and it upset me very much. We had an instant rapport. He had no right to get this disease. Who exactly does he think he is? *(Grace's light goes out. A light comes up on Todd.)*

TODD. It was not uncommon to see my mother in her girdle and bra. This was a natural thing. The bra was trans-lucent and I could see her nipples through the fabric. This was considered dressed. Or maybe it was just OK to see my mother's nipples. I never saw Emma's nipples. I saw my father's nipples plenty of times. I assume my mother did. And when he saw my nipples, it was strictly by chance, and not very often ... *(Todd's light goes out. A light comes up on Tommy, carrying a polishing rag.)*

TOMMY. I didn't grow up with these people. I'm not part of this family and I think any memories I'd have of the nuns and priests at the orphanage would be inappropriate. *(General light comes up. Tommy goes to the dinosaur skeleton, now one-third finished and standing on a platform. He polishes it. Emma enters.)*

EMMA. Stop that!

TOMMY. I promised your brother —

EMMA. How can you touch it! It's a carcass!

TOMMY. Think of it as sculpture.

EMMA. *(Going to him.)* Take me away!

TOMMY. What?

EMMA. Let's run away. We can go to Las Vegas! They have chapels in malls.

TOMMY. What are you talking about?

EMMA. I don't want to live here anymore!

TOMMY. What about my job?

EMMA. Quit!

TOMMY. Your mother's been so good to me.

EMMA. You won't help me. I hate you.

TOMMY.   I thought you loved me.

EMMA.   I do — I mean — I want to get away! We don't have to get married. We'll live in a field!

TOMMY.   There are bugs.

EMMA.   We'll eat them! We'll make them into a paste and spread them like jam!

TOMMY.   I don't care for bugs.

EMMA.   *(Loosing control.)* I have to get away! There's a crack in the plaster over my bed, over my body and it's getting worse! One night it'll snap and I'll snap with it! We have to go! My parents are apes! They talk in code! In riddles! I hate my dress! It's either too big or too small! And I never seem to change it! I'm trapped in my dress! I'm a prisoner—

TOMMY.   Shut up! *(He grabs her.)*

EMMA.   Help me!

TOMMY.   You're pretty. *(He grabs her nipple.)*

EMMA.   OUCH! *(He clubs her to the floor with a grunt. There is a blackout. Todd rushes into a pool of light and addresses the audience.)*

TODD.   Earlier, when I gave my overview of life on the planet, I explained that I'd forgotten my notes. Now, it's been pointed out to me that I made some mistakes. But I'm not going to correct them, because I don't believe they were mistakes. I think the people who corrected me are idiots. The point is, I forgot my favorite part. The ten plagues. I love the plagues. They happened, as you know, or maybe you don't, after the Jews built the pyramids, or before it, or during. And God wanted to punish the Egyptians for being nasty to the Hebrews, so he tortured them with plagues. I don't remember them all. There was lice and vermin, which always seemed redundant to me. And frogs and blood and something else and something else. And my favorite, the slaying of the first born. It's my favorite because I am a "first born." *(Solemn.)* "And it came to pass at midnight, that the Lord smote all the first born in the land of Egypt, from the first born of the Pharaoh that sat upon the throne unto the first born of the captive in the dungeon; and all the first born of the cattle. And Pharaoh rose up in the night, he and all his servants,

and all the Egyptians; and there was a great cry in the land of Egypt; for there was not a house where there was not one dead. And he called for Moses and Aaron by night and said: 'Rise up and get you forth from among my people, both ye and the children of Israel; and go and serve the Lord as ye have said.' And the Egyptians were urgent to send them out of the land in haste; for they said ... 'We are all dead men.'"
(The lights come up. All are present. Todd goes to work on the dinosaur. Arthur is reading the newspaper. Emma holds an ice pack on her breast. Tommy cleans windows.)

GRACE.   *(Blankly.)* Let's talk funerals.

ARTHUR.   Grace!

GRACE.   Well since Todd is dying —

TOMMY.   Did you ever see *Funeral in Berlin*?

ARTHUR.   Buzz isn't dying.

TODD.   I have no symptoms.

EMMA.   *(Raising her hand.)* I have symptoms.

GRACE.   I thought he might want to have some say — come away from that thing.

ARTHUR.   It's revolting.

TODD.   It's our history.

GRACE.   I want to talk to you.

TOMMY.   I like it.

TODD.   It's a stegosaurus.

EMMA.   It's icky.

TODD.   Or a tyrannosaurus.

EMMA.   It's creepy

TODD.   Or a coelurosaurus.

EMMA.   It's Roget's *Thesaurus!*

TOMMY.   With a shade, in the corner, and a forty-watt bulb —

GRACE.   Don't you want some say in what happens after you're gone?

ARTHUR.   I find this inappropriate.

TODD.   *(Still working.)* In terms of what?

ARTHUR.   *(To Todd.)* Let's have a catch! Ya like that, Buzzboy?

TODD. No.

GRACE. In terms of who reads what, who wears what —

ARTHUR. We'll go in the yard. It's your day!

TODD. Did you know dinosaurs lived as families, traveling in packs?

ARTHUR. Who cares?

EMMA. The air is like sand.

GRACE. *(To Todd.)* What would you like to wear?

TOMMY. I'd like to wear something simple with a —

ARTHUR. *(To Tommy, hostile.)* Isn't it dinnertime?

TOMMY. Excuse me. *(Tommy exits.)*

ARTHUR. *(Going to Emma.)* Let's plan the wedding!

EMMA. *(Politely.)* Please don't touch me.

ARTHUR. I think that's a good idea! It's okay with you, isn't it, Buzzboy?

TODD. Todd.

GRACE. I'll wear my black Donna Karan.

EMMA. At my wedding?

GRACE. It's very simple. A black column. Very Greek. Very tragic. Very Medea.

ARTHUR. I don't think that's appropriate.

EMMA. It's my wedding.

ARTHUR. People will talk.

EMMA. I wish I were dead.

GRACE. I love planning a party!

ARTHUR. Grace.

GRACE. Or an affair.

EMMA. *(To Todd.)* Can you breathe?

TODD. Yes.

GRACE. Emma, you wear that new black Romeo Gigli.

EMMA. I thought I'd wear white.

ARTHUR. And you'll look beautiful.

EMMA. What do you mean by that?

GRACE. How's "Oh, Promise Me?"

ARTHUR. At Buzz's funeral?

TODD. I'm not dying.

GRACE. At Emma's wedding.

TODD. Did you know all dinosaurs lived on land?

GRACE. I thought that's what you wanted to plan.

TODD. Pterodactyls, for instance, weren't dinosaurs. They lived in the sky. But they died just the same.

GRACE. *(To Todd.)* Open casket?

ARTHUR. Stay on one subject Grace.

GRACE. *(Out.)* I love planning a party! The occasion is piffle.

EMMA. The air is like halvah.

GRACE. Remember the party I threw for the new lawn jockey?

EMMA. Of course not.

ARTHUR. Remember that, Buzz?

TODD. Call me Todd.

ARTHUR. Remember that?

GRACE. I thought we might do something along those lines.

TODD. At her wedding?

EMMA. At his funeral?

ARTHUR. Grace! No one knows what you're talking about!

GRACE. Don't shout at me!

TODD. Don't bully her!

ARTHUR. Don't be fresh, Buzz.

TODD. My name is Todd!

EMMA. *(Extending her hand.)* My name is Emma. Have we met?

TODD. *(To Emma, hostile.)* Christ!

ARTHUR. It's all right, Emma.

EMMA. *(Politely.)* Please don't touch me.

GRACE. What about entertainment?

TODD. I'll read poems by Brecht!

EMMA. At my wedding?

GRACE. Too downbeat.

TODD. His comic poems.

GRACE. I thought a sit-down dinner, on the lawn, under a tent.

TODD.   I like this one:
  I am dirt. From Myself
  I can demand nothing but
  Weakness, treachery and degradation.*
ARTHUR.   That's not comic. Not remotely.
GRACE.   I thought squab or salmon, or both with pearl on-
ions!
TODD.   How about:
  With arsenic: I had
  Tubes in my side with
  Pus flowing night and day —*
EMMA.   Ick!
GRACE.   Emma, if you have a hundred can Tommy make
do with a hundred?
TODD.   Should I continue?
GRACE, ARTHUR and EMMA.   No!
EMMA.   A hundred what?
GRACE.   Guests. People. Friends. Family.
EMMA.   Tommy has no family.
TODD.   Lucky.
EMMA.   And I have no friends.
TODD.   What about Alice Paulker?
EMMA.   Dead.
ARTHUR.   I cannot afford dinner for two hundred people!
GRACE.   How many weddings will you give?
EMMA.   I don't need a wedding.
GRACE.   Yes, you do.
EMMA.   I don't I don't I don't.
GRACE.   How many daughters do you have?
EMMA.   (Panicked.) Are there sisters I've repressed?
ARTHUR.   Who are these two hundred people?
GRACE.   There are the Beatons and the Litwilers and the
Hamners and the Seatons —
ARTHUR.   I loathe Nora Beaton!
GRACE.   You do not!

* See Special Note on Poems on copyright page.

ARTHUR.   She's a Buddhist!

GRACE.   That's Cora Seaton!

EMMA.   Coriciden is a cold medication.

GRACE.   You like Nora Beaton.

EMMA.   My sinuses hurt.

GRACE.   You ought to. You slept with her.

ARTHUR.   Grace!

GRACE.   Think back. Eight years ago, Pearl Harbor day?

ARTHUR.   What are you talking about?

GRACE.   In the gardener's shed!

ARTHUR.   I have no idea —

GRACE.   I knew it! Everyone knew it!

TODD.   I never knew.

EMMA.   I might have known it.

GRACE.   No one cared!

EMMA.   *(Out.)* I would have repressed it.

GRACE.   I never cared.

ARTHUR.   Because you were drunk!

TODD.   Leave her alone.

ARTHUR.   Be quiet Buzz.

GRACE.   I don't get drunk!

ARTHUR.   You don't even know it!

TODD.   I said —

ARTHUR.   Buzz!

GRACE.   I've never been drunk!

ARTHUR.   You get drunk and you forget!!

TODD.   I said —

ARTHUR.   Be quiet Buzz!! *(Todd explodes in a rage which shocks the others.)*

TODD.   MY NAME IS TODD!!!!!

GRACE.   My God —

TODD.   WHY CAN'T YOU CALL ME TODD!!!? WHY CAN'T YOU CALL ME BY MY NAME!!!?

ARTHUR.   It's a nickname —

TODD.   IT IS NOT!!!

GRACE.   Your father doesn't mean —

TODD.   IT IS SOMEONE ELSE'S NAME!! MY NAME IS TODD!!

EMMA.   Means death in German.

TODD.   BUZZ IS THE NAME OF AN ASTRONAUT! I DON'T KNOW ANYONE NAMED BUZZ OR BUZZY OR BUZZBOY!! MY NAME IS TODD!

ARTHUR.   You're overwrought —

GRACE.   MY SON IS DYING!!

TODD.   I AM NOT DYING!!

ARTHUR.   This can't be healthy —

GRACE.   I'M BEING PUNISHED! GOD IS PUNISHING ME!!

TODD.   I WILL NOT DIE! I WILL NOT! I WILL BE HERE FOREVER! WHEN YOU ARE DUST I WILL BE HERE! I WILL OUTLIVE THE TREES AND THE STARS AND THE SEAS AND THE PLANET! I AM DIRT AND FROM MYSELF I CAN DEMAND NOTHING! I AM THE AIR AND I WILL BE HERE WHEN THE AIR IS GONE! WHEN THE EARTH FALLS OUT OF ITS ORBIT I WILL GO ON! WHEN THE SEAS MERGE AND SWALLOW THE LAND I WILL GO ON! WHEN THERE IS NOTHING I WILL GO ON! I WILL GO ON I WILL GO ON I WILL GO ON I WILL GO ON I WILL GO ON!!! *(Tommy enters.)*

TOMMY.   Dinner is served! *(Blackout. We hear a bright, too-cheery song such as "Ac-cent-tchu-ate the Positive."*)*

---

*   See Special Note on Music on copyright page.

ACT TWO

Scene 1

"An Appropriate Gift"

A pool of light comes up on Grace, who addresses the audience.

GRACE.   When Todd came home and told me what had happened to him, told me of his illness, I studied him. I watched him with the devotion of a Carmelite Nun. I listened for any irregularity in my child's breathing. I scrutinized his diet. I made a job of noticing his weight, his mood and the way his clothes hung on him from one day to the next. Was he walking slower? Was his speech lethargic? Did he sleep, enough? But ... his gate was quick, his speech unchanged and he slept through the night. *(As she continues a light comes up on the dinosaur skeleton, now obviously a Tyrannosaurus, more than half finished, it towers over the room, up C.)* He devoted himself to his work. He was driven and I was glad, because it gave him a purpose. And I realized that my concern, might be interpreted, by him, as panic. I was afraid he would hate me for having no faith, when he had so much. And there, as a tribute to his will, stood my child's grotesque monument to the transience of everything. So with the frenzy of a dervish, I threw myself into other things. *(The lights come up, revealing Emma, on the sofa, writing thank you notes, wearing a cocktail length wedding dress. Gifts are scattered about. Through the French doors we see that it is Autumn. Grace fiddles with the place cards.)*
EMMA.   How do you spell "escargot?"
GRACE.   All the place cards are out of order.
EMMA.   You don't know how to spell escargot?
GRACE.   Thirty-two is man heavy.
EMMA.   What does that mean?

GRACE. It's all men. How did that happen?

EMMA. What difference does it make?

GRACE. Good God, Emma. It makes all the difference — who on earth sent you snails?

EMMA. Not snails, Mother. Forks. Escargot forks. Two dozen.

GRACE. From whom?

EMMA. Cousin Paul.

GRACE. Typical. Never marries. Sends forks.

EMMA. I like Cousin Paul. I think he's funny.

GRACE. Oh he's funny all right.

EMMA. "... love, Emma." Can I stop now?

GRACE. How many have you done?

EMMA. Forty-two. And I have writer's block.

GRACE. *(Shuffling cards.)* You mean writer's cramp — If I put Louise at thirty-two, I can put David Cumstock at eleven.

EMMA. Can I change please?

GRACE. Let me see the hem. *(As Emma rises, Tommy enters from outdoors.)*

TOMMY. Has anyone called for me?

EMMA. Shut your eyes! Shut your eyes!

TOMMY. Have they?

EMMA. You're not supposed to see me before the wedding!

TOMMY. I see you when I shut my eyes.

GRACE. Isn't that sweet?

TOMMY. Has anyone called?!

GRACE. Tommy, would you mind not sitting with Emma, tomorrow?

TOMMY. No.

EMMA. I'd mind.

GRACE. Have you tried on your tux?

TOMMY. Has anyone called!?

EMMA. No.

GRACE. You're going to look dashing in pants.

TOMMY. Thank you.

GRACE. And isn't Emma's dress beautiful? I'm so glad we decided against the full-length. Is the hem straight?

TOMMY. The hem?

EMMA. I can't breathe.

TOMMY. I think so.

GRACE. I hope I ordered enough champagne.

EMMA. You did.

GRACE. Well, do me a favor and don't drink champagne.

EMMA. At my wedding?

GRACE. Drink Scotch.

EMMA. I don't like Scotch.

GRACE. You haven't given it a chance. Trust me, drink enough of it, you'll like it. *(Phone rings. Tommy rushes to answer it.)*

TOMMY. Hello.... It's for you. *(He hands the phone to Grace.)*

GRACE. Hello? Oh, hello, Mr. Lavie.

EMMA. Where were you all morning?

TOMMY. Out.

EMMA. Out. Out? Out? Out where?

TOMMY. I had some errands to run.

EMMA. What does that mean?

GRACE. *(Into the phone.)* Oh, that is too bad —

TOMMY. I had things to do.

EMMA. What kind of things?

TOMMY. Personal things. Private things.

GRACE. *(Into the phone.)* No. I don't understand —

EMMA. You have secrets. I hate secrets.

TOMMY. I don't have secrets. I have boundaries.

EMMA. I hate them more. Boundaries make me feel insecure. They make me feel unworthy of being loved. Boundaries make me feel fat.

TOMMY. Don't be stupid.

EMMA. Name calling makes me feel needy and unwanted.

TOMMY. I'm sorry. I'm just nervous.

GRACE. *(Into the phone.)* That simply won't do. *(Hangs up.)* This is terrible!

EMMA. What is it Mother?

GRACE. That was Mr. Lavie. There's a problem with the rabbit pâté.

TOMMY. Rabbit pâté?

GRACE. For the cocktail hour — it seems all the rabbits

had cervical cancer and the pâté is contaminated.

TOMMY. Ick.

EMMA. I don't like the idea of eating bunnies anyway.

GRACE. That leaves us short on hors d'oeuvres! What am I supposed to do? Pass out Ritz crackers?

EMMA. I like Ritz crackers!

GRACE. I hate Mr. Lavie! He wears a pinkie ring with a diamond in it. And did you see? The tent is mustard and navy! I specifically asked for burnt ochre and midnight!

TOMMY. What's burnt ochre?

EMMA. Mustard.

GRACE. The orchids are heliotrope!

TOMMY. What's heliotrope?

EMMA. Purple.

GRACE. They look like giant bruises! I ordered aubergine!

TOMMY. What's aubergine?

EMMA. Purple.

GRACE. It's all part of the harvest — the vegetable theme I'm doing. The ochre, the aubergine — it's a visual cornuco-pia — *(The phone rings, Grace answers it.)* Hello?

TOMMY. Is it for me?

GRACE. *(Waving him away.)* Oh hello dear!

TOMMY. You were right. I'm sorry we didn't elope.

GRACE. *(Into the phone.)* That is too bad. Of course I under-stand. I'll call you soon. Bye, bye. *(She hangs up the phone.)* I hate her !!!!

EMMA. Who's that?

GRACE. Nina Triten!

EMMA. Who?

GRACE. You remember her, from the club.

EMMA. No.

GRACE. Well, she begs me to have her children at the wed-ding — you know I hate children, socially, at an affair — but she begs me. She plays the devoted mother, can't leave them home, can't leave them with strangers. So I acquiesce. And now, when it's too late to fill her table, she cancels! She and her six, screaming, sticky-fingered little brats!

EMMA. Why?

GRACE. Oh I don't know. I wasn't listening. Something about death, cancer, lymphoma, one of her children. Who cares? It was obviously an excuse!

TOMMY. Cancer?

GRACE. I should just throw the place cards in the air and start from scratch. Twenty-seven is empty! I could put your father O'Hara there, and the Gideon twins — I know! Tommy, do you think if I called them right now, eight or nine of those Nuns who raised you might be free tomorrow?

TOMMY. I don't know.

GRACE. Of course they are. What else do they have to do all day?

TOMMY. They supplicate.

GRACE. Oh, they can skip that for one day. This is an emergency. God won't mind — I better go through my address book — Oh why does everything happen to me? *(Grace exits up the stairs.)*

EMMA. I have something to tell you.

TOMMY. Then just tell me! Do you have to narrate everything you do? Can't you just do things? It's not normal.

EMMA. I'm pregnant.

TOMMY. What?

EMMA. I'm going to have a baby.

TOMMY. Who's the father?

EMMA. You are of course! I knew something was happening to me. My colon wasn't hurting and my leg stopped cramping.

TOMMY. Those aren't signs.

EMMA. And I missed my last two periods. The doctor called this morning. Do you want to feel it?

TOMMY. No thank you.

EMMA. Your seed is growing inside of me. I hope it's a boy. Or a girl! I love children. Don't you?

TOMMY. No.

EMMA. What do you mean?

TOMMY. What could I mean by "no?"

EMMA. Children are nice.

TOMMY. Noisy, screaming bundles of goo.

EMMA. You'll come around. No one likes children until they have one.

TOMMY. We'll see.

EMMA. Tomorrow we'll leave here and never come back.

TOMMY. Don't you think we should stay until the baby comes.

EMMA. Why?

TOMMY. You don't know anything about babies.

EMMA. There's nothing to know. My breasts'll make milk.

TOMMY. I just think —

EMMA. You promised me!

TOMMY. I know I did.

EMMA. I can't stay here! It's been all right! I've been all right because I knew I was escaping! I knew there was an end!

TOMMY. I don't want to go.

EMMA. *(Not listening to him.)* Todd scares me! He's creepy. He spends all of his time with the bones of dead things! And my father's possessed — I know it! He speaks in tongues!

TOMMY. Don't be dramatic.

EMMA. I don't let on because I don't want him to eat me! He comes to me at night. He wears a halo of fire. His feet are cloven, his hair is a tangle of snakes and his tongue is a mile long!

TOMMY. Your father?

EMMA. I can't breathe!

TOMMY. Mr. Duncan?

EMMA. You promised you'd save me!!

TODD. *(Offstage.)* Hello.

EMMA. *(To Tommy.)* CHEESE IT! *(Todd enters, carrying books on dinosaurs and a gift. To Todd, cheery.)* Hello.

TODD. You look very beautiful in your dress.

EMMA and TOMMY. Thank you.

TODD. I meant Emma.

TOMMY. Oh.

EMMA. Thank you.

TODD. Although you look well too, Tommy.

TOMMY. This old thing?

49

EMMA.   I had another memory today! We were in a beautiful hot air balloon, with tiny twinkling lights on the basket, listening to "Moonlight Serenade."

TODD.   That never happened.

EMMA.   But I remember it.

TODD.   I've never been in a hot air balloon.

TOMMY.   That's from the cult-favorite, much maligned, 1980 Woody Allen film, *Stardust Memories.*

TODD.   (*Out.*) Never saw it.

TOMMY.   (*Out.*) Self indulgent.

EMMA.   (*Out.*) Guess I liked it.

TOMMY.   How are you feeling?

TODD.   Fine.

EMMA.   It's remarkable that you have no symptoms.

TODD.   I brought you a gift.

EMMA.   I love presents! What's the occasion?

TODD.   Your wedding.

TOMMY.   It's very nice of you.

EMMA.   (*Unwrapping it.*) It's beautiful! It's ... a gun.

TODD.   Your pattern.

EMMA.   It's sweet. It's a sweet looking gun.

TODD.   I hope you like it.

EMMA.   It's lovely, but, do you really think a gun is an appropriate gift?

TODD.   I didn't know what to get you.

EMMA.   I like earrings.

TOMMY.   Don't be ungrateful.

EMMA.   It's pretty!

TODD.   (*Taking the gun, loading it.*) I thought you might need it.

EMMA.   And we don't have a gun. Do we honey?

TODD.   I thought since you're leaving —

EMMA.   You told him?! I can't believe you told him!

TOMMY.   I didn't mean to. It slipped out.

EMMA.   We promised we wouldn't.

TOMMY.   He won't tell anyone.

EMMA.   That's not the point! We agreed!

TOMMY.   Well I did it and I can't undo it!

TODD.   You'll need it out there. Everything is ending. People are corpses. They trample each other and never notice the cry of sorrow. While mothers, doctors, and civilized men practice their genocide.

EMMA.   *(Bewildered, retrieving the gun.)* Well ... I'll just go toss this in my hope chest. *(Emma exits.)*

TOMMY.   I'm going to die.

ARTHUR.   *(Enters and hangs his jacket on the dinosaur.)* Grace! Where's Mrs. Duncan? Grace!

TODD.   I've asked you not to do that!!!

TOMMY.   *(Removing it.)* I'll take it sir.

ARTHUR.   How are you feeling Buzz-Todd?

TODD.   Fine!

ARTHUR.   No symptoms?

TODD.   No! *(Phone rings. Tommy rushes to it, dropping Arthur's jacket on the floor. Todd goes to work on the dinosaur.)*

TOMMY.   Hello?

ARTHUR.   Where's your Mother?

TODD.   Upstairs.

ARTHUR.   Grace!

TOMMY.   *(Irritated, into the phone.)* Oh, just a minute. *(Grace enters.)*

GRACE.   Is that you Arthur? What are you doing home? Isn't it the afternoon? I've lost the thread of the day —

TOMMY.   *(Handing Grace the phone.)* It's for you.

GRACE.   Thank you, Tommy. Hello?

TOMMY.   Can I get you something, Sir?

ARTHUR.   Privacy.

GRACE.   *(Into the phone.)* You must be kidding me.

TOMMY.   *(Hostile.)* I'm just doing my job.

GRACE.   *(Hanging up.)* This is terrible!

TOMMY.   What is it?

GRACE.   Arthur, can you play the violin?

ARTHUR.   Of course not.

GRACE.   Viola?

ARTHUR.   Grace!

GRACE.   It seems our violinist was killed this morning by a stray bullet during a bank hold-up.

TOMMY.   Did he work at a bank?

GRACE.   He was holding one up.

ARTHUR.   Who cares? No one'll miss one violin from an orchestra.

GRACE.   It's a string quartet.

TODD.   Not any more.

ARTHUR.   I have to talk to you Grace.

GRACE.   *(Starting to rush off.)* Can't it wait? I have to locate a violin and practice like mad.

ARTHUR.   No! Something terrible has happened.

GRACE.   Oh I know it. The tent is wrong, the flowers are off, the rabbits' malignant and I've got a table full of nuns at twenty-seven.

ARTHUR.   *(Sitting.)* Get me a drink.

TOMMY.   *(Bitterly.)* Yes'm Massa Duncan. *(Tommy exits.)*

GRACE.   I wish, Arthur, you'd say please to the servants. Your curtness is read as ingratitude. You're the reason we can't keep good help.

ARTHUR.   Don't criticize me. I've had a terrible day.

GRACE.   So have I. See your set-backs as challenges. That's what I do.

TODD.   I had a nice day.

GRACE.   Did you?

TODD.   But I see my set-backs as set-backs.

ARTHUR.   Please. I don't know how to say this — *(Tommy enters with a drink.)*

TOMMY.   Here.

ARTHUR.   Why are you still wearing that?

TOMMY.   It's my uniform.

ARTHUR.   I asked you to wear pants.

TOMMY.   Mrs. Duncan said —

ARTHUR.   It's awful.

GRACE.   It's snappy.

ARTHUR.   It's faggy.

GRACE.   Arthur, please.

ARTHUR.   Well, it is. It's the fruitiest thing I've ever seen.

GRACE.   *(Under her breath.)* You'll offend Todd.

ARTHUR.   Oh, he doesn't care. Do you Buzz-Todd?

GRACE.　Arthur, he's homosexual.

ARTHUR.　That doesn't mean he's effeminate.

GRACE.　He'll have another "fit."

ARTHUR.　That's all behind ya, isn't it Buzz-Todd?

TODD.　No.

TOMMY.　I think I look like Tony Curtis in *Some Like It Hot!*

ARTHUR.　I hated that movie.

TOMMY.　*(Hostile.)* It's a classic.

GRACE.　*(To Arthur.)* You never had a sense of humor.

TODD.　I found it politically incorrect in its portrayal of transvestites as buffoons.

GRACE.　Didn't you have something to tell me? I left Emma on a stool upstairs with pins in her hem.

ARTHUR.　Don't look at me. I don't think I can say this if anyone is looking at me. *(The others turn away from Arthur.)*

GRACE.　Oh my. Maybe I should have a drink too.

ARTHUR.　What?

GRACE.　It sounds as if I'm going to need one.

ARTHUR.　Do you have to?

GRACE.　Just one.

ARTHUR.　It always starts with "just one," doesn't it?

GRACE.　*(Turning back to Arthur.)* What does?

ARTHUR.　You know very well.

GRACE.　I don't know what you're talking about — Tommy, a scotch. *(Tommy rises.)*

ARTHUR.　Sit down, Tommy. *(Tommy sits.)* I'm asking you not to.

GRACE.　If I understood your implication, I'd be insulted. A drink, please. *(Tommy rises.)*

ARTHUR.　Sit Tommy. *(Tommy sits.)*

GRACE.　Stand Tommy. *(Tommy rises.)*

ARTHUR.　Grace, it's not even four.

GRACE.　So what?

ARTHUR.　If you start now, you'll be gone by dinner.

GRACE.　Gone? Gone where? Try to avoid the vague euphemism.

TOMMY.　Would you like me to leave?

ARTHUR.　That would be best. *(Tommy starts to exit.)*

53

GRACE. Stay put Tommy. (*Tommy sits.*) If Mr. Duncan wishes to hurl ugly accusations, let him do so in public. What are you trying to say, Arthur?

ARTHUR. You're an alcoholic, Grace.

GRACE. (*Very still.*) What did you say to me?

TODD. He called you an alcoholic.

ARTHUR. I wish you wouldn't drink so much!

GRACE. What's "so much?"

ARTHUR. You drink yourself blind every night.

GRACE. You call that "so much?" Please.

ARTHUR. Your drinking is out of control!

GRACE. I don't have a problem! Todd! Am I an alcoholic?

TODD. Of course.

GRACE. Speak up.

TODD. Yes. You're an alcoholic.

GRACE. Oh piffle! I don't have a problem! You're the one with the problem, Arthur!

ARTHUR. I know this is a difficult time. We're all under alot of strain. Buzz-Todd's sick. There's a big dead thing in the living room —

GRACE. (*Snapping.*) You wouldn't know if I were drinking or dying — (*To Todd.*) Sorry.

ARTHUR. Fine! I don't want to discuss it!

GRACE. I could have left you years ago and you'd never know it! You're never here!

ARTHUR. I'm always here —

GRACE. Were you home for dinner last night? Or the night before?

TOMMY. I slave and slave over a hot stove.

ARTHUR. Well, why bother! You'd be passed out in the tub!

GRACE. Were you!

ARTHUR. I was working!!

TOMMY. Likely excuse.

ARTHUR. Night and day! To satisfy your insatiable need for "things!"

GRACE. You delude yourself Arthur! You always have. Justify your philandering! I'm a drunk so you can assuage your guilt over being less than a father and less than a husband. But I've told you Arthur, your indiscretion is immaterial to me. I learned a long time ago to replace you in my affections, as you had me in yours. Now! What did you want to tell me?

ARTHUR. *(Sweetly, cruel.)* It pains me to say this, Grace. But the fact is, I no longer have a job. *(Pause.)*

GRACE. Pardon me?

ARTHUR. That's it. That's what I wanted to tell you. It's over. It's all over. Finished. Done.

GRACE. *(Still stunned.)* What are you talking about?

ARTHUR. I have been asked to step down.

GRACE. Well, decline politely!

ARTHUR. It's not that simple.

GRACE. You're the president Arthur!

ARTHUR. Was dear. Was the president. Past tense.

GRACE. You're lying.

ARTHUR. Why would I lie about a thing like this?

GRACE. This is a dream. I'm living a dream —

ARTHUR. It's no dream. It's over. And I must say, I feel so free. I feel comfortable for the first time.

GRACE. *(Simply.)* What happened?

ARTHUR. It's complicated.

GRACE. Explain it to me!

ARTHUR. In time.

GRACE. Now!

ARTHUR. I feel as if a terrible burden has been lifted. I feel lighter.

GRACE. How dare you?

ARTHUR. It wasn't my choice Grace.

GRACE. Women I could tolerate. Not poverty!

ARTHUR. We can spend more time together.

GRACE. *(After a moment, a threat.)* What did you do?

ARTHUR. *(Not recognizing the word.)* Do? I'm sorry.

GRACE. You were at that bank for thirty years!

ARTHUR. Good years.

GRACE. You were president for ten!

ARTHUR. Wonderful years.

GRACE.   Things don't just happen — you did something!

ARTHUR.   I did my best.

GRACE.   Did you steal? Did you embezzle?

ARTHUR.   I feel positively liberated.

GRACE.   STOP SAYING THAT.

ARTHUR.   So sorry. Buzz-Todd, a catch?

TODD.   No, thank you.

ARTHUR.   Aw.

GRACE.   You did something! I know it! You did this on purpose! This has been a terrible goddamn — did you see that tent!!? — EXCUSE ME!!

ARTHUR.   *(After a moment.)* I think that went very well.

TODD.   What did you do?

ARTHUR.   I didn't do anything.

TODD.   Don't lie to me. I can tell.

ARTHUR.   I need some air. *(Arthur exits onto the terrace. Todd turns to the dinosaur.)*

TODD.   I'm almost finished.

TOMMY.   I'm going to die.

TODD.   You said that.

TOMMY.   I'm scared!

TODD.   Everybody dies. Grow up.

TOMMY.   I've been to the doctor.

TODD.   Doctors are sadists.

TOMMY.   I've had a blood test.

TODD.   Doctors are idiots.

TOMMY.   He should call.

TODD.   What difference does it make?

TOMMY.   It makes a difference to me!

TODD.   You blame me don't you?

TOMMY.   I want to.

TODD.   *(Working on the dinosaur.)* Do you realize some species of dinosaur cannibalized themselves?

TOMMY.   But I love you

TODD.   Did you know the brachiosoraus ate the eggs of its young?

TOMMY.   No I didn't! I said I love you!

TODD.   Lower your voice. Someone'll hear you.

TOMMY.   I don't care! I'm going to die, what do I care who hears me? You're the only thing that matters to me now.
TODD.   That's extremely flattering.
TOMMY.   Look at me!
TODD.   *(Does so.)* You can live a long time. You can live forever with this disease.
TOMMY.   I dreamed, last night, that I was dying.
TODD.   Me too.
TOMMY.   You dreamed you were dying?
TODD.   No. I dreamed you were.
TOMMY.   Creepy.
TODD.   You were in a forest.
TOMMY.   That's right.
TODD.   You were choking. You were drowning. You were coughing. It was awful.
TOMMY.   And you held me.
TODD.   No. I wasn't there.
TOMMY.   *(Grabbing Todd.)* Don't do this to me!
TODD.   Let go of me!
TOMMY.   I need you! It's my own fault, I knew what I was doing, and I didn't care! I wanted it. Every night, I decided. But please ... say I matter. Stay with me. *(Tommy is distraught. In a rare moment of softness, Todd comforts him.)*
TODD.   All right. It's all right. *(They embrace.)*
TOMMY.   My life was a series of random accidents. Now everything seems ordered.
TODD.   Avoid clichés.
TOMMY.   You make me happy? *(They kiss. Emma rushes down the stairs.)*
EMMA.   Mother, are you ever — oh my. *(Tommy and Todd break their embrace. Phone. Emma answers it.)* Hello?
TOMMY.   Is that for me?
EMMA.   *(Into the phone.)* No, this is her daughter.
TODD.   I'll leave the two of you alone.
TOMMY.   Don't.
EMMA.   *(Into the phone.)* Yes. I'll tell her, crab claws. Thank you. *(She hangs up.)* Tommy? What, um, was going on, before, when I came down the stairs? What was happening?

TOMMY.   Well, Emma, I was kissing your brother. And I'm glad you came in. I don't want to hurt you — But I have to be honest. And the truth is, I love Todd. I'm in love with Todd.

EMMA.   What? Huh? What? What?

TOMMY.   I said I'm in love with Todd.

EMMA.   *(After a moment, gaily.)* I'M DEAF!

TOMMY.   What?

EMMA.   I AM! I'M DEAF! I'M STONE COLD DEAF!

TOMMY.   Don't play games.

EMMA.   I KNOW YOU'RE TALKING. I CAN SEE YOUR LIPS MOVING AND YOUR CHEST IS GOING UP AND DOWN —

TODD.   Let me try.

EMMA.   FUNNY HOW IT JUST COMES OVER A GIRL.

TODD.   EMMA! EMMA! CAN YOU HEAR ME? CAN YOU HEAR ME EMMA?

EMMA.   *(Banging her ears.)* HUH? HUH? WHAT? WHAT? WHAT?

TODD.   She's faking.

TOMMY.   Really?

TODD.   She hears you. She's faking.

TOMMY.   What should I do?

TODD.   Just talk. She hears you.

EMMA.   WHAT? WHAT ARE YOU SAYING? ARE YOU TALKING TO ME?

TOMMY.   EMMA. I'M SORRY.

EMMA.   WAIT! WAIT! WAIT!

TOMMY.   SAY YOU UNDERSTAND.

EMMA.   I HEAR SOMETHING!

TOMMY.   SAY YOU FORGIVE ME.

EMMA.   I HEAR A SONG!

TODD.   SHE HEARS YOU.

EMMA.   A Johnny Mercer song. Or Hoagy Charmical! I ALWAYS GET THEM CONFUSED.

TOMMY.   I CAN'T MARRY YOU. BUT I'LL ALWAYS CARE ABOUT YOU. YOU'RE A KIND SWEET INSANE PERSON AND I HOPE YOU FIND WHO YOU'RE LOOKING FOR.

EMMA. *(Continuing in good cheer.)* I HOPE YOU DON'T MIND THAT I'M DEAF. I KNOW SOME MEN WOULD BUT SOME WOULD LIKE IT. IT WON'T MATTER. KNOW WHY? BECAUSE WE LOVE EACH OTHER AND OUR LOVE CAN SUSTAIN DEAFNESS! WE'RE GOING TO BE SO HAPPY! *(Grace enters from the kitchen, drink in hand, wickedly bright.)*

GRACE.   LET'S REHEARSE! *(Emma doesn't respond. She is deaf.)*

TOMMY.   We've got to talk, Mrs. Duncan —

GRACE.   Tomorrow you travel from servant to son, call me Grace —

TOMMY.   But —

GRACE.   *(To Todd.)* Where's your father?

TODD.   Out there.

GRACE.   Be a cherub and get him. Go, go, go, go, go. *(Todd exits onto the terrace.)*

TOMMY.   You don't understand Mrs. Duncan.

GRACE.   Grace means beauty of form, proportion and movement, please address me thus.

TOMMY.   All right, Grace, it's about the wedding —

GRACE.   Which needs the nurturing and attention of a hothouse orchid. *(Todd and Arthur enter from the terrace.)*

ARTHUR.   What is it?

GRACE.   We're going to rehearse!

ARTHUR.   Rehearse what, for God's sake?

GRACE.   The wedding, you squid.

ARTHUR.   Have you been drinking?

GRACE.   I am naturally gregarious!! Now, tomorrow morning —

TOMMY.   Listen to me!

GRACE.   We'll talk later.

TODD.   There's no judge.

GRACE.   He can wing it —

TOMMY.   MRS. DUNCAN!

GRACE.   Oh what is it!?

TOMMY.   There's not going to be a wedding.

GRACE.   What?

ARTHUR.   Thank god.

TOMMY.   I'm sorry, but the wedding is off.

GRACE.   Emma! What do you have to say about this? *(In response, Emma stands and bursts into a grotesquely cheerful performance of "Skylark"* by Hoagy Charmical and Johnny Mercer. She continues to sing under the dialogue, until her exit.)* What? What does that mean?

ARTHUR.   What's wrong with her?

TOMMY.   She seems to be deaf.

ARTHUR.   Oh my God! My baby!

TODD.   She hears music.

TOMMY.   Johnny Mercer.

ARTHUR.   Pumpkin.

GRACE.   Oh that's nothing. That's hysterical deafness. I had it on my wedding day.

ARTHUR.   Can you hear me?

GRACE.   It's nothing. — Now, Emma you go upstairs and come down during "Here Comes The Bride." Todd, you be the judge over there by the terrace. Emma go upstairs. Arthur you stand on the stairs and take Emma when she passes. Emma go now. I'll have come down first in my Christian LaCroix and I'll join Todd, by the judge at the door — Arthur just push her, she'll go — *(Arthur starts Emma with a push. She exits, upstairs, Grace continues her high-speed directions.)* Tommy, you enter from the kitchen, with your best man, that Father O'Hara and go directly to the judge, who's Todd, and Todd, and myself.

TOMMY.   I don't love your daughter! I can't marry her! The wedding is off!

GRACE.   *(After a moment.)* There will be a wedding! You listen to me! Two hundred and fifty people — eight of them nuns — are descending on this house tomorrow, and you can trust me, they will be treated to a wedding! A beautiful, expensive and excessive affair! Thirteen kinds of hors d'oeuvres! Aubergine orchids, burnt ochre strips and a string trio playing "La Vie En Rose"!!

---

* See Special Note on Music on copyright page.

TOMMY.   But I don't love her —

GRACE.   So what!!! As you may or may not have heard, for reasons passing understanding, I am about to be stripped of the amenities to which I've grown accustomed! Plunged into poverty! And this wedding, this social event, this bacchanalian carnival of rapacious consumption shall be my last hurrah! My fond farewell to all I care about, need, love and have worked for all my life! So mark my words, there will be a wedding!! PLACES!!!! *(As they scatter to their places, in fear, Grace maniacally sings Mendelssohn's "Wedding March.")* Da da da da! Da da da — *(The phone rings.)*

TOMMY.   I'll get it!!!

GRACE.   STAY. *(She answers the phone.)* Hello?

TOMMY.   Is that for me?

GRACE.   *(Into the phone.)* He can't. I'll take a message.

TOMMY.   *(Kneeling at her feet.)* Give me the phone!

GRACE.   *(Into the phone, cheery.)* Blood test positive. Thank you doctor, okydoke. *(She hangs up the phone.)*

TOMMY.   Oh my God.

GRACE.   *(Turning to the stairs.)* EMMA! *(Singing.)* Da da da da! Da da da da! Da da da da da da da — *(There is a gunshot. Todd steps out of the scene, into a pool of light.)*

TODD.   And then it got very, very cold. *(Lights shift as Todd and Tommy exchange a look of farewell.)*

Scene 2

"A Walk in the Park"

The lights come up on Todd and the dinosaur, now complete, a giant skeleton towering over the room. Todd addresses the audience.

TODD.   And it was a Tyrannosaurus Rex. Named from the Latin, meaning king lizard. And it was the largest land-living carnivore who walked the earth. And it was beautiful. He lived in the Cretaceous period of the Mesozoic era, one hundred and fifty million years ago. He is recognized by his large head, small forelimbs, and dagger-like teeth. He started life at fifty pounds and grew to sixty tons, unless he died, as mine, a child for reasons no one can remember, because no one was alive. *(Todd curls up under the dinosaur. The general lighting comes up, revealing the room, no longer grand, but gray and dreary. Outside it is winter. There is a bottle of Scotch and a glass on the end table. Grace enters from the kitchen, her dress is now threadbare. She wears an afghan around her shoulders. Her high-flown chatter has been replaced with an alcoholic snarl. She carries a bowl of cereal and a spoon. She sits. She holds the bowl to her ear and listens.)*

GRACE.   Damn. I've been robbed.

TODD.   What?

GRACE.   *(To the Dinosaur.)* What?

TODD.   You said something.

GRACE.   I didn't know you were there.

TODD.   What'd you say?

GRACE.   You want to keep me company?

TODD.   What did you say?

GRACE.   I asked if you want to keep me company.

TODD.   Before that.

GRACE.   Oh. I said, I've been robbed.

TODD.   What are you talking about?

GRACE.   My cereal is supposed to make noise.

TODD.   Like music?

GRACE.   Like popping or something.

TODD.   *(Going to her.)* You're eating cornflakes.

GRACE.   So?

TODD.   Rice Crispies make noise. Cornflakes are silent.

GRACE.   Oh ... how's your fever?

TODD.   Normal.

GRACE.   Is it cold in here?

TODD.   No.

GRACE.   Check the thermostat.

TODD.   The thermostat's broken.

GRACE.   Maybe I'm going through the change.

TODD.   If you were going through "the change" you'd have
hot flashes, not cold flashes.
GRACE.   Are you a gynecologist?
TODD.   No.
GRACE.   You're a woman then?
TODD.   No.
GRACE.   Then what would you know about menopause?
TODD.   *(Starting to exit.)* I'm going upstairs.
GRACE.   No don't. Keep me company. I miss everybody.
TODD.   You never liked them to begin with.
GRACE.   I like you.
TODD.   Thanks.
GRACE.   We're so much alike.
TODD.   So you say —
GRACE.   We have the same interests —
TODD.   So often.
GRACE.   We have the same temperament. We like the same
things.
TODD.   Stop saying that.
GRACE.   The same music. The same kind of people.
TODD.   I'm not you. I'm me. I'm not like you. I'm like me.
GRACE.   You see? It would drive me crazy too — if some-
one kept saying I were like them.
TODD.   *(Snapping at her.)* Can we talk about something else?
GRACE.   I always change the subject. Typical.
TODD.   *(Going up the stairs.)* I'm going upstairs.
GRACE.   I go upstairs! See? You see?
TODD.   Mother!
GRACE.   I'm sorry. I won't do it anymore. I'll just sit and
eat my cornflakes.
TODD.   Good.
GRACE.   *(After a moment.)* I miss Emma.
TODD.   *(Returning.)* Did you like her?
GRACE.   Of course. What do you mean?
TODD.   I don't.
GRACE.   Don't what?
TODD.   Miss her.
GRACE.   She was your sister.

TODD.   I know that — How long have you been drinking?
GRACE.   Twenty years.
TODD.   I meant today.
GRACE.   So did I.
TODD.   You better eat your cornflakes.
GRACE.   I hate them.
TODD.   Well, you're supposed to add milk.
GRACE.   We didn't have any.
TODD.   Well, no wonder you can't eat them.
GRACE.   Why don't you miss your sister?
TODD.   I don't know —
GRACE.   Do you miss Tommy?
TODD.   Who?
GRACE.   Tommy. Tommy. The maid. Tommy.
TODD.   Oh. I suppose.
GRACE.   Me too.
TODD.   He was a good maid.
GRACE.   We'd have milk.
TODD.   It's true.
GRACE.   *(Going to the window.)* He went so fast. It was sad. It's good he choked, drowned. He got so ugly, all purple and swollen. *(She turns and looks out the window. She focuses on something specific, then quickly turns back to Todd.)* We should bury him Todd.
TODD.   The ground is frozen.
GRACE.   Come look at him.
TODD.   I'd rather not.
GRACE.   He looks so sad.
TODD.   Naturally he looks sad. He's dead.
GRACE.   We should bury him.
TODD.   The ground's too hard.
GRACE.   It's not right.
TODD.   Who sees him?
GRACE.   That's not the point!
TODD.   If no one sees him, it doesn't matter!
GRACE.   It's not right —
TODD.   What does that mean?!
GRACE.   You know what I mean!

TODD.   You think God cares?

GRACE.   He shouldn't just be lying there.

TODD.   You want him buried?! You bury him!

GRACE.   Don't shout at me!

TODD.   Don't nag me!

GRACE.   Leave me alone!

TODD.   I'm going upstairs. *(Todd starts to exit, but stays on the stairs and sits. He watches the scene. Grace pours herself a drink. Emma enters from the terrace and addresses the audience.)*

EMMA.   Hello everybody. I'm dead. How are you? I'm glad I killed myself. I'm not recommending it for others, mind you — no Dr. Kevorkian am I. But it's worked out for me. Looking back, I don't think I was ever supposed to have been born to begin with. Of course the idea that anything is "supposed to be," implies a master plan, and I don't believe in that kind of thing. When I say, I shouldn't have been born, I mean that my life was never all that pleasant. And there was no real reason for it. I was pretty. I had money. I was lucky enough to be born in a time and into a class where I had nothing but opportunities. I look around and there are crippled people and blind people and refugees and I can't believe I had the gall to whine about anything! I had my health — oh sure, I complained alot, but really I was fine. And I had love! Granted the object of my affections was a latent, or not-so latent homosexual as it turned out, who was infected with the HIV virus, who in turn infected me and my unborn baby — but isn't that really picking nits? I can never thank Todd enough for giving me the gun, because for the first time, I'm happy. The pain is gone and I remember everything. Tommy is here, but we're not speaking. He spends all his time with Montgomery Clift and George Cukor talking about movies. I assume. And I've been reunited with Alice Paulker. We went to school together. She was shot last year by a disgruntled postal worker. She has long, wavy brown hair and skin so pale you can see right through it — I don't mean it's really transparent and you can see her guts and organs and everything. It's just pale. And she has very big eyes, green. And we listen to music and go for walks. We take turns reading aloud to each other. She reads poems by Emily Brontë and I read chapters from the *The Tropic of Cancer,* by Henry Miller. She was always classier than me. And sometimes, we don't read. Sometimes, we just hold each other. And I run my fingers through her hair and she touches her lips, gently, along my cheek. She makes soft sounds, comforting sounds and she takes her time and runs her tongue along the edge of my ear. We take off our clothes and just look at each other. I was shy at first, but Alice helped me and never rushed me. She held my breasts in her hands and ran her lips between them, down my stomach. I touch her eyelids and her forehead and her hair and her fingers and the back of her neck. And she enters me and I am everywhere at once and nowhere at all. And I remember everything and find that nothing matters. And for a moment, for a moment or two that lasts forever, we become one person. And I forget, we forget, that we were ever alive. And everything makes perfect sense. (*Emma joins Todd on the stairs. Arthur enters from the terrace, wearing a winter coat, which he quickly removes.*)

ARTHUR.   It's freezing in here.

GRACE.   Where've you been?

ARTHUR.   I went for a walk.

GRACE.   Why?

ARTHUR.   I wanted to.

GRACE.   You know you're not supposed to.

ARTHUR.   Supposed to?

GRACE.   You want to catch pneumonia?

ARTHUR.   Just for you. This year, for Christmas.

GRACE.   Very funny.

ARTHUR.   I wore a coat.

GRACE.   It doesn't matter. It's zero out. It's zero degrees.

ARTHUR.   I didn't notice.

GRACE.   You wander around outside in the zero degrees like some kind of goddamn polar bear —

ARTHUR.   I thought it was warm.

GRACE.   What?

ARTHUR.   I was warm.

GRACE.   Did you eat today?

ARTHUR.   Of course I ate —

GRACE.   You forget to eat and —

ARTHUR.   I'm perfectly fine. I ate! It's warm out.

GRACE.   It's freezing.

ARTHUR.   It's spring.

GRACE.   It's December.

ARTHUR.   It can't be.

GRACE.   It is.

ARTHUR.   But the sun was hot. The birds are crying for water.

GRACE.   There aren't any birds, Arthur.

ARTHUR.   You're lying.

GRACE.   Birds go south in the winter, Arthur. God, where were you in the third grade?

ARTHUR.   Don't be snide with me Grace.

GRACE.   I give up.

ARTHUR.   I accept that birds go south in the winter. I know that. I'm not a child. What I do no accept, is your basic premise that it IS winter. How could it be? I was just outside on the steaming lawn. You're trying to drive me insane!

GRACE.   And doing very well.

ARTHUR.   It's obviously spring or at the very latest, summer.

GRACE.   *(Starting to exit.)* I'll fix you something to eat.

EMMA.   *(From her place.)* I love you Daddy.

ARTHUR.   Wait a minute, Grace.

GRACE.   What is it?

ARTHUR.   We should talk about the wedding.

GRACE.   What do you want to eat Arthur?

EMMA.   I don't need a wedding.

ARTHUR.   Is everything ready?

GRACE.   Do you want a sandwich? Do you want some eggs?

ARTHUR.   It has to be beautiful.

GRACE.   What does?

ARTHUR.   The wedding.

GRACE.   It was months ago — or actually, it wasn't.

ARTHUR.   I'll be nice, on the lawn —

GRACE.   I mean it would have been.

ARTHUR.   Under the trees. Under a tent.

GRACE. There was no wedding, Arthur. You know that.

ARTHUR. Is everything ready?

GRACE. I told you yesterday. I told you this morning.

ARTHUR. Everything should be perfect.

GRACE. I told you at lunch.

ARTHUR. Every detail.

GRACE. Emma is gone, Arthur.

EMMA. *(Out.)* Death is a walk in the park.

ARTHUR. What do you mean. Did she run away?

GRACE. No. I mean she's dead.

ARTHUR. Pardon me?

GRACE. She was dead yesterday. Dead this morning. Dead last night and she'll be dead tomorrow.

ARTHUR. Don't be ridiculous — *(He calls upstairs.)* EMMA! EMMA! *(Emma would respond, but Todd stops her.)*

GRACE. *(After a moment.)* You see?

ARTHUR. Maybe she's out?

GRACE. She's not.

ARTHUR. She's napping.

GRACE. She's not.

ARTHUR. She's sleeping.

GRACE. She's dead.

ARTHUR. Very deeply?

GRACE. She shot herself.

ARTHUR. I don't feel well.

GRACE. I'll get you an aspirin. *(Grace exits. Arthur addresses the audience.)*

ARTHUR. When she was a girl, Emma wanted to be a sports announcer on the radio. She loved the Philadelphia Phillies. She talked about them all the time. She said their names over and over again.

EMMA. *(Out.)* I wanted to be a ballerina.

ARTHUR. Nick Etten, Danny Litwiler, Eddy Waitkus.

EMMA. *(Out.)* Or a nurse.

ARTHUR. And her favorite, Granville Hamner.

EMMA. *(Out.)* Or a wife and mother.

ARTHUR. She worshipped him.

TODD. *(Standing.)* That's not true.

ARTHUR.   What?

EMMA.   *(Out.)* But I don't really like children.

TODD.   What you're saying isn't true.

EMMA.   So it's for the best.

ARTHUR.   What would you know about it?

TODD.   *(Descending the stairs.)* That's what you say about me.

ARTHUR.   I have a headache.

TODD.   But it's not true.

ARTHUR.   Let's have a catch? Would you like that?

TODD.   About anyone. *(Grace re-enters with an aspirin.)*

GRACE.   Here you are — Todd, what are you doing up?

TODD.   I couldn't sleep.

ARTHUR.   We're going to have a catch.

TODD.   We'd die from the cold.

EMMA.   *(Out.)* I hate crowds.

GRACE.   Take a pill Arthur.

ARTHUR.   I don't want to take a pill.

GRACE.   Too bad.

TODD.   He was saying how Emma liked the Phillies.

GRACE.   You liked the Phillies, Arthur.

ARTHUR.   I did?

GRACE.   *(To Todd.)* Maybe you should lie down.

TODD.   I don't want to lie down.

ARTHUR.   *(To Todd.)* Did you like the Phillies?

TODD.   I hate baseball.

EMMA.   *(Out.)* Me too.

GRACE.   No one likes baseball, Arthur.

ARTHUR.   What are you talking about? Lots of people like baseball! It's the national pastime!

GRACE.   No one in the room.

ARTHUR.   Who are you people?

GRACE.   I'm your wife.

TODD.   And your son.

ARTHUR.   I miss Emma.

GRACE.   Well, too bad. She's gone.

TODD.   Say dead.

ARTHUR.   *(To Todd.)* And it's your fault!

GRACE.   He didn't kill her!

ARTHUR.   He gave her the gun!

GRACE.   Leave him alone —

ARTHUR.   Why should I?

GRACE.   Because he's sick!

TODD.   I'm fine!

GRACE.   *(To Todd.)* Go to bed!

ARTHUR.   Someone has to be responsible!

GRACE.   She's responsible. She did it.

ARTHUR.   She wouldn't.

EMMA.   *(Out.)* I did.

TODD.   But she did.

GRACE.   She did it herself.

ARTHUR.   I blame you!

GRACE.   *(To Todd.)* Go. To. Bed.

EMMA.   *(Out.)* To get away.

ARTHUR.   I hate you!

GRACE.   Arthur!

TODD.   I know.

GRACE.   *(To Todd.)* He doesn't mean that —

ARTHUR.   I do!

GRACE.   *(To Arthur.)* He's sick!

TODD.   I'M NOT!

ARTHUR.   She wouldn't leave me all alone!

EMMA.   Sure, I would.

GRACE.   You're not alone Arthur! What the hell's the matter with you? I'm here —

TODD.   Me too.

GRACE.   I was here in the beginning, I'm still here! I will always be here!

ARTHUR.   But I don't love you Grace.

GRACE.   *(After a long pause.)* Oh.

ARTHUR.   I loved Emma. She was beautiful.

EMMA.   Thank you.

ARTHUR.   She was perfect.

TODD.   And you wanted to fuck her.

ARTHUR.   NO!! THAT IS NOT TRUE!!

GRACE.   *(Panicked.)* Let's talk about dinner.

TODD.   You killed her. Leering at her, staring at her, touch-

ing her —
GRACE.   Is anyone hungry?
ARTHUR.   I NEVER DID ANYTHING WRONG!!
EMMA.   That's debatable.
TODD.   Kissing her—
ARTHUR.   WHY ARE YOU HERE!
TODD.   I have no one —
GRACE.   He's our child!
TODD.   I belong here.
ARTHUR.   YOU DO NOT BELONG HERE!
GRACE.   Of course he does!
TODD.   Where then?
ARTHUR.   I DON'T CARE. I'M SORRY, BUT I DON'T!
GRACE.   Stop it Arthur! Stop this!
ARTHUR.   I DO NOT WANT YOU HERE! I DON'T
KNOW YOU AND YOU DON'T BELONG! MY LIFE WAS
GOOD — MY LIFE WAS — I DON'T WANT YOU HERE!

TODD.   Too Fucking bad! Too bad for you! What do you want?! Some pretty family! Pretty wife! Pretty daughter! Pretty son named BUZZ! TOO FUCKING BAD! BUZZ IS GONE! BUZZ IS DEAD! BUZZ NEVER WAS!

ARTHUR.   I don't care what happens! Where you go — I do not care! I DON'T! YOU'RE NOT MY CHILD! GET AWAY! STOP IT! STOP IT! STOP IT!

(Arthur attacks Todd. There is a struggle. Arthur is strangling Todd.)
GRACE and EMMA.   Stop! *(Arthur stops, realizes what he's done. He walks away, slowly.)*
EMMA.   *(Out.)* Death is a day at the beach.
GRACE.   *(At Todd's side.)* Are you all right?
TODD.   I'm fine.
ARTHUR.   I'm sorry.
TODD.   I'm fine.
ARTHUR.   I don't know ...
GRACE.   *(To Arthur, stunned.)* What's wrong with you?
ARTHUR.   I don't know.

71

TODD.　He tried to kill me.

ARTHUR.　I lost control.

GRACE.　*(Standing.)* I think you should go.

ARTHUR.　What?

GRACE.　I think you should leave.

ARTHUR.　I'm you husband.

GRACE.　Just go. *(Arthur starts to exit.)*

ARTHUR.　*(After a moment, to Todd.)* You're to blame. *(Arthur exits.)*

GRACE.　You're all right?

TODD.　Yes.

GRACE.　You want to lie down? *(Todd shakes his head "no.")*

TODD.　You don't believe him, do you?

GRACE.　What about?

TODD.　I'm not to blame.

GRACE.　Of course not. You're my baby. *(Todd pours Grace a drink.)* Thank you.

TODD.　It'll be dark soon.

GRACE.　Are you hungry?

TODD.　No.

GRACE.　You have to keep up your strength.

TODD.　I'm not hungry.

GRACE.　Let me know. I'll cook you something. *(She downs her drink.)*

TODD.　You can't cook.

GRACE.　I know it. Do you remember, when you were little? We'd have canned carrots for dinner. That was it. On cook's day off, we'd have carrots and I'd call that dinner.

TODD.　I remember.

GRACE.　You didn't mind. Never cared about food. Really. Just like me. You and I are just alike.

TODD.　I suppose.

GRACE.　Always were.

TODD.　And it's a shame.

GRACE.　What is?

TODD.　You made me just like yourself, when you hate yourself to begin with.

GRACE.　You'll give me a headache.

TODD. Sorry. *(He fills her glass. A light goes out, then another, reducing their playing area. Grace is very tired and somewhat drunk.)*

GRACE. It's so cold.

TODD. It'll be dark soon.

GRACE. Are you hungry?

TODD. No.

GRACE. You have to keep up your strength. *(She drinks.)*

TODD. I feel fine.

GRACE. You are amazing. You are so strong. My Baby ... how long has it been?

TODD. Since what?

GRACE. Since your father left?

TODD. I don't know. Two weeks. A month.

GRACE. Really?

TODD. Why'd you marry him?

GRACE. I hate it when it's dark in here. At night.

TODD. I like it.

GRACE. It gets so dark. I feel like I'm floating in space. I feel completely alone. Like I was the last living thing on earth.

TODD. That's why I like it.

GRACE. Play with my hair.

TODD. No. *(He fills her glass. Another light goes out, reducing their playing space further. Grace is groggy, and quite drunk, very broken and disoriented.)*

GRACE. It's so cold. *(She downs her drink.)*

TODD. It's almost dark.

GRACE. Let me look at you.

TODD. What do you want?

GRACE. I just want to look at you. I want to look at my baby. I hate your disease.

TODD. I don't.

GRACE. You're so beautiful.

TODD. I have no symptoms.

GRACE. I'll cook you something. *(She tries, unsuccessfully, to rise.)*

TODD. Sit down.

GRACE. I got dizzy.

73

TODD. Lie down.

GRACE. *(She does so.)* I'm so sleepy.

TODD. Take a nap.

GRACE. You have to eat. Can't let you die.

TODD. I think I died a long time ago.

GRACE. What does that mean? *(Todd puts the afghan over her.)*

TODD. Take a nap.

GRACE. Some mothers don't love their children. But you know I do, don't you?

TODD. Yes.

GRACE. Love me?

TODD. Of course.

GRACE. Talk to me. Maybe I'll sleep if you talk to me.

TODD. What about?

GRACE. I don't care. Dinosaurs.

TODD. Two hundred and twenty million years ago the dinosaurs came to be. And they were large. In comparison to man they were. And they lived not in harmony, roaming the earth at will, raping as it were, the planet. But they cared for their young and they flourished as no creature before or since, for one hundred and fifty million years before dying out completely. And no one knows why. Why they lived. Or ceased to. Some people think there was a meteor. Perhaps volcanic ash altered the atmosphere. Some think they overpopulated and the shells of their eggs became too thin. Or they just ran their course, and their end was the order of things. And no tragedy. Or disease. Or God. *(He looks at Grace. He covers her face with the afghan. She is dead.)* It's so dark. *(He exits up the stairs. When he reaches Emma, they embrace. Then they walk together, up the stairs. Once they are gone, the lights dim, but for the light on the skeleton, which grows brighter and brighter.)*

CURTAIN

PROPERTY LIST

ACT ONE

ON STAGE:
Telephone
Small bell
Message pad and pen by phone
Emma's purse with bottle of Darvon inside
Blanket (hidden under sofa, for flashback)
Dinosaur skeleton, half finished
Letter opener

OFF STAGE:
Easel with map and pointer (TODD)
Purse, with compact (GRACE)
Various shopping bags (GRACE)
Large canvas bag with bones inside (TODD)
Drinking glasses with drink (GRACE)
Dinosaur skull (TODD)
Feather duster (TOMMY)
Dust cloth (TOMMY)
Additional bones (TODD)
Dinosaur books (TODD)
Sick of gum (ARTHUR)
Ice pack (EMMA)
Mixing bowl and whisk (TOMMY)

ACT TWO

ON STAGE:
Various gifts, wrapped and unwrapped
Seating chart
Place cards
Box of thank you notes

Completed thank you notes
Silver pen
Vase of purple orchids
Dinosaur skeleton, complete

OFF STAGE:
Gift wrapped gun (TODD)
Trench coat (ARTHUR)
Glasses of Scotch (ARTHUR, TOMMY, GRACE)
Bottle of Scotch (GRACE)
Ratty afghan (GRACE)
Bowl of dry cornflakes (GRACE)
Spoon (GRACE)

COSTUME PLOT

ACT ONE

TODD
Oversized jacket (distressed)
Denim shirt (distressed)
T-shirt (distressed)
Baggy chinos (distressed)
Tan socks
Bown belt (distressed)
Brown work shoes (distressed)

EMMA
Navy/white polka dot dress
Pearl earrings
Pearl necklace
Natural hose
Ivory pumps

TOMMY
Blue blazer (optional)
Oxford shirt
Chinos
Sneakers
Black belt
Maid's uniform (dress, apron)

GRACE
Purple dress
Sunglasses
Crystal necklace
Natural hose
Beige pumps
Wedding band
Engagement ring
Tapestry purse (with matching glasses case)
Earrings

Black slacks
Purple sash belt
Forest green blouse
Jet necklace
Black hose
Black pumps
Lavender bathrobe
Lavender slippers

ARTHUR
Tan suit (jacket, trousers)
Striped shirt
Patterned tie
Suspenders
Tan dress socks
Cordivan shoes
Navy suit
Striped shirt
Striped tie
Suspenders
Navy dress socks
Black shoes

ACT TWO

Scene 1

TODD
Same as Act One, add pajama top worn as jacket

TOMMY
Same as Act One, add windbreaker

GRACE

Purple pants suit (Pollazo pants, blouse with flounce)
Vest
Necklace (ivory or crystal)
Natural hose
Bracelet
Purple pumps

ARTHUR
Gray suit, pinstripe
Navy/red striped tie
White shirt
Navy socks
Black shoes
Suspenders

EMMA
Cocktail-length wedding dress
Natural hose
Ivory pumps
Pearl earrings

Scene 2

TODD
Same as Scene 1, exchange pajama top for cardigan

GRACE
Mauve bathrobe
Mauve pajamas
Slippers

ARTHUR
Winter coat
Muffler
Brown corduroy pants
Beige shirt (distressed)

Brown socks
Brown shoes
Olive cardigan

EMMA
Cream dress
Cream hose
Cream pumps

SOUND EFFECTS

Telephone ring
Gun shot

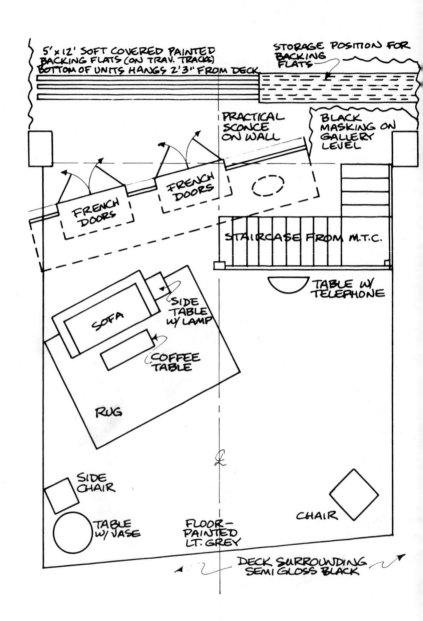

SCENE DESIGN

"PTERODACTYLS"

(DESIGNED BY JAMES YOUMANS FOR VINEYARD THEATRE)

NEW PLAYS

★ **MONTHS ON END by Craig Pospisil.** In comic scenes, one for each month of the year, we follow the intertwined worlds of a circle of friends and family whose lives are poised between happiness and heartbreak. "...a triumph...these twelve vignettes all form crucial pieces in the eternal puzzle known as human relationships, an area in which the playwright displays an assured knowledge that spans deep sorrow to unbounded happiness." *–Ann Arbor News.* "...rings with emotional truth, humor...[an] endearing contemplation on love...entertaining and satisfying." *–Oakland Press.* [5M, 5W] ISBN: 0-8222-1892-5

★ **GOOD THING by Jessica Goldberg.** Brings us into the households of John and Nancy Roy, forty-something high-school guidance counselors whose marriage has been increasingly on the rocks and Dean and Mary, recent graduates struggling to make their way in life. "...a blend of gritty social drama, poetic humor and unsubtle existential contemplation..." *–Variety.* [3M, 3W] ISBN: 0-8222-1869-0

★ **THE DEAD EYE BOY by Angus MacLachlan.** Having fallen in love at their Narcotics Anonymous meeting, Billy and Shirley-Diane are striving to overcome the past together. But their relationship is complicated by the presence of Sorin, Shirley-Diane's fourteen-year-old son, a damaged reminder of her dark past. "...a grim, insightful portrait of an unmoored family..." *–NY Times.* "MacLachlan's play isn't for the squeamish, but then, tragic stories delivered at such an unrelenting fever pitch rarely are." *–Variety.* [1M, 1W, 1 boy] ISBN: 0-8222-1844-5

★ **[SIC] by Melissa James Gibson.** In adjacent apartments three young, ambitious neighbors come together to discuss, flirt, argue, share their dreams and plan their futures with unequal degrees of deep hopefulness and abject despair. "A work...concerned with the sound and power of language..." *–NY Times.* "...a wonderfully original take on urban friendship and the comedy of manners—a *Design for Living* for our times..." *–NY Observer.* [3M, 2W] ISBN: 0-8222-1872-0

★ **LOOKING FOR NORMAL by Jane Anderson.** Roy and Irma's twenty-five-year marriage is thrown into turmoil when Roy confesses that he is actually a woman trapped in a man's body, forcing the couple to wrestle with the meaning of their marriage and the delicate dynamics of family. "Jane Anderson's bittersweet transgender domestic comedy-drama ...is thoughtful and touching and full of wit and wisdom. A real audience pleaser." *–Hollywood Reporter.* [5M, 4W] ISBN: 0-8222-1857-7

★ **ENDPAPERS by Thomas McCormack.** The regal Joshua Maynard, the old and ailing head of a mid-sized, family-owned book-publishing house in New York City, must name a successor. One faction in the house backs a smart, "pragmatic" manager, the other faction a smart, "sensitive" editor and both factions fear what the other's man could do to this house— and to them. "If Kaufman and Hart had undertaken a comedy about the publishing business, they might have written *Endpapers*...a breathlessly fast, funny, and thoughtful comedy ...keeps you amused, guessing, and often surprised...profound in its empathy for the paradoxes of human nature." *–NY Magazine.* [7M, 4W] ISBN: 0-8222-1908-5

★ **THE PAVILION by Craig Wright.** By turns poetic and comic, romantic and philosophical, this play asks old lovers to face the consequences of difficult choices made long ago. "The script's greatest strength lies in the genuineness of its feeling." *–Houston Chronicle.* "Wright's perceptive, gently witty writing makes this familiar situation fresh and thoroughly involving." *–Philadelphia Inquirer.* [2M, 1W (flexible casting)] ISBN: 0-8222-1898-4

DRAMATISTS PLAY SERVICE, INC.
440 Park Avenue South, New York, NY 10016 212-683-8960 Fax 212-213-1539
postmaster@dramatists.com www.dramatists.com

NEW PLAYS

★ **BE AGGRESSIVE by Annie Weisman.** Vista Del Sol is paradise, sandy beaches, avocado-lined streets. But for seventeen-year-old cheerleader Laura, everything changes when her mother is killed in a car crash, and she embarks on a journey to the Spirit Institute of the South where she can learn "cheer" with Bible belt intensity. "...filled with lingual gymnastics...stylized rapid-fire dialogue..." –*Variety*. "...a new, exciting, and unique voice in the American theatre..." –*BackStage West*. [1M, 4W, extras] ISBN: 0-8222-1894-1

★ **FOUR by Christopher Shinn.** Four people struggle desperately to connect in this quiet, sophisticated, moving drama. "...smart, broken-hearted...Mr. Shinn has a precocious and forgiving sense of how power shifts in the game of sexual pursuit...He promises to be a playwright to reckon with..." –*NY Times*. "A voice emerges from an American place. It's got humor, sadness and a fresh and touching rhythm that tell of the loneliness and secrets of life...[a] poetic, haunting play." –*NY Post*. [3M, 1W] ISBN: 0-8222-1850-X

★ **WONDER OF THE WORLD by David Lindsay-Abaire.** A madcap picaresque involving Niagara Falls, a lonely tour-boat captain, a pair of bickering private detectives and a husband's dirty little secret. "Exceedingly whimsical and playfully wicked. Winning and genial. A top-drawer production." –*NY Times*. "Full frontal lunacy is on display. A most assuredly fresh and hilarious tragicomedy of marital discord run amok...absolutely hysterical..." –*Variety*. [3M, 4W (doubling)] ISBN: 0-8222-1863-1

★ **QED by Peter Parnell.** Nobel Prize-winning physicist and all-around genius Richard Feynman holds forth with captivating wit and wisdom in this fascinating biographical play that originally starred Alan Alda. "QED is a seductive mix of science, human affections, moral courage, and comic eccentricity. It reflects on, among other things, death, the absence of God, travel to an unexplored country, the pleasures of drumming, and the need to know and understand." –*NY Magazine*. "Its rhythms correspond to the way that people—even geniuses—approach and avoid highly emotional issues, and it portrays Feynman with affection and awe." –*The New Yorker*. [1M, 1W] ISBN: 0-8222-1924-7

★ **UNWRAP YOUR CANDY by Doug Wright.** Alternately chilling and hilarious, this deliciously macabre collection of four bedtime tales for adults is guaranteed to keep you awake for nights on end. "Engaging and intellectually satisfying...a treat to watch." –*NY Times*. "Fiendishly clever. Mordantly funny and chilling. Doug Wright teases, freezes and zaps us." –*Village Voice*. "Four bite-size plays that bite back." –*Variety*. [flexible casting] ISBN: 0-8222-1871-2

★ **FURTHER THAN THE FURTHEST THING by Zinnie Harris.** On a remote island in the middle of the Atlantic secrets are buried. When the outside world comes calling, the islanders find their world blown apart from the inside as well as beyond. "Harris winningly produces an intimate and poetic, as well as political, family saga." –*Independent (London)*. "Harris' enthralling adventure of a play marks a departure from stale, well-furrowed theatrical terrain." –*Evening Standard (London)*. [3M, 2W] ISBN: 0-8222-1874-7

★ **THE DESIGNATED MOURNER by Wallace Shawn.** The story of three people living in a country where what sort of books people like to read and how they choose to amuse themselves becomes both firmly personal and unexpectedly entangled with questions of survival. "This is a playwright who does not just tell you what it is like to be arrested at night by goons or to fall morally apart and become an aimless yet weirdly contented ghost yourself. He has the originality to make you feel it." –*Times (London)*. "A fascinating play with beautiful passages of writing..." –*Variety*. [2M, 1W] ISBN: 0-8222-1848-8

DRAMATISTS PLAY SERVICE, INC.
440 Park Avenue South, New York, NY 10016 212-683-8960 Fax 212-213-1539
postmaster@dramatists.com www.dramatists.com

NEW PLAYS

★ **SHEL'S SHORTS by Shel Silverstein.** Lauded poet, songwriter and author of children's books, the incomparable Shel Silverstein's short plays are deeply infused with the same wicked sense of humor that made him famous. "…[a] childlike honesty and twisted sense of humor." –*Boston Herald.* "…terse dialogue and an absurdity laced with a tang of dread give [*Shel's Shorts*] more than a trace of Samuel Beckett's comic existentialism." –*Boston Phoenix.* [flexible casting] ISBN: 0-8222-1897-6

★ **AN ADULT EVENING OF SHEL SILVERSTEIN by Shel Silverstein.** Welcome to the darkly comic world of Shel Silverstein, a world where nothing is as it seems and where the most innocent conversation can turn menacing in an instant. These ten imaginative plays vary widely in content, but the style is unmistakable. "…[*An Adult Evening*] shows off Silverstein's virtuosic gift for wordplay…[and] sends the audience out…with a clear appreciation of human nature as perverse and laughable." –*NY Times.* [flexible casting] ISBN: 0-8222-1873-9

★ **WHERE'S MY MONEY? by John Patrick Shanley.** A caustic and sardonic vivisection of the institution of marriage, laced with the author's inimitable razor-sharp wit. "…Shanley's gift for acid-laced one-liners and emotionally tumescent exchanges is certainly potent…" –*Variety.* "…lively, smart, occasionally scary and rich in reverse wisdom." –*NY Times.* [3M, 3W] ISBN: 0-8222-1865-8

★ **A FEW STOUT INDIVIDUALS by John Guare.** A wonderfully screwy comedy-drama that figures Ulysses S. Grant in the throes of writing his memoirs, surrounded by a cast of fantastical characters, including the Emperor and Empress of Japan, the opera star Adelina Patti and Mark Twain. "Guare's smarts, passion and creativity skyrocket to awesome heights…" –*Star Ledger.* "…precisely the kind of good new play that you might call an everyday miracle…every minute of it is fresh and newly alive…" –*Village Voice.* [10M, 3W] ISBN: 0-8222-1907-7

★ **BREATH, BOOM by Kia Corthron.** A look at fourteen years in the life of Prix, a Bronx native, from her ruthless girl-gang leadership at sixteen through her coming to maturity at thirty. "…vivid world, believable and eye-opening, a place worthy of a dramatic visit, where no one would want to live but many have to." –*NY Times.* "…rich with humor, terse vernacular strength and gritty detail…" –*Variety.* [1M, 9W] ISBN: 0-8222-1849-6

★ **THE LATE HENRY MOSS by Sam Shepard.** Two antagonistic brothers, Ray and Earl, are brought together after their father, Henry Moss, is found dead in his seedy New Mexico home in this classic Shepard tale. "…His singular gift has been for building mysteries out of the ordinary ingredients of American family life…" –*NY Times.* "…rich moments …Shepard finds gold." –*LA Times.* [7M, 1W] ISBN: 0-8222-1858-5

★ **THE CARPETBAGGER'S CHILDREN by Horton Foote.** One family's history spanning from the Civil War to WWII is recounted by three sisters in evocative, intertwining monologues. "…bittersweet music—[a] rhapsody of ambivalence…in its modest, garrulous way…theatrically daring." –*The New Yorker.* [3W] ISBN: 0-8222-1843-7

★ **THE NINA VARIATIONS by Steven Dietz.** In this funny, fierce and heartbreaking homage to *The Seagull*, Dietz puts Chekhov's star-crossed lovers in a room and doesn't let them out. "A perfect little jewel of a play…" –*Shepherdstown Chronicle.* "…a delightful revelation of a writer at play; and also an odd, haunting, moving theater piece of lingering beauty." –*Eastside Journal (Seattle).* [1M, 1W (flexible casting)] ISBN: 0-8222-1891-7

DRAMATISTS PLAY SERVICE, INC.
440 Park Avenue South, New York, NY 10016 212-683-8960 Fax 212-213-1539
postmaster@dramatists.com www.dramatists.com